DAUGHTERS OF
HANNAH
&
ELKANAH

Mary and Mariah

KAREN SOBEK

To order additional copies of this book, contact:
Xlibris
1-888-795-4274
www.Xlibris.com
Orders@Xlibris.com

World English Bible with Deuterocanonical/Apocryphal & Hebrew Names Version updated version of American Standard Version Bible, copyrighted 1901 Philip Schaff translation, published by Thomas Nelson, N.Y. Public Domain

ISBN: Softcover   978-1-7960-5449-1
         Hardcover   978-1-7960-5450-7
         EBook   978-1-7960-5448-4

Print information available on the last page

Rev. date: 08/30/2019

Dedicated Out of Love
to
God Almighty Amen Elyon Most High God Yahweh
and the Holy Family Hannah & Elkanah and their children
Samuel, Abijah, Eliezar, Mary and Mariah
and to
All the Prophets and Seers of God Almighty

INTRODUCTION

God in all His infinite wisdom had all the Prophets and Seers write all that was said, and done in history to form books to preserve the truth. God Bless the Prophets, and Seers for obeying God Almighty Yahweh for these books were preserved to form the Torah, the books of the Old Testament. God had stated that all truth would be revealed in the end.

Many people don't even realize that Constantine had Eusebius rewrite history, as contained within the New Testament, to glorify the emperors and the Roman empire. The gospels were just fragments, and could not justify the common era to glorify Rome. This Roman religion was built on a created logos name of a messiah from three to four different cults myths from Egyptian Ra and his son Horus, Isis, Persian Mithra, Babylonian Ishtar, India's Krishna myths that believed in a trinity of pagan gods. This formed the basis of their Roman one world religion, and the concept of paganism in a trinity of gods. Roman sol invictus is the worship of the sun god, and his son, developed from pagan myths to form a logos name of iesus (jesus) christos.

In my other book, "I AM Amen Yahweh Yashar'El, Your Savior, Your King," goes into more depth of information on this Roman concept of a one world religion, and how over centuries made people believe, through repetition of those lies, into thinking that the New Testament was a basis of truth. There have been many books that were destroyed by evil over the centuries, just like Hitler burned books, and was in unison with the Vatican to keep people from learning the truth. Many of these books from antiquities were either destroyed, or hidden away in Vatican secret archives, which would have further established that the historical events occurred in antiquities of the Old Testament.

My book, is my humble effort to bring to light this truth, not for the glory of myself, but for the Glory of God Almighty Yahweh, and the Blessed Mother Mary. For my love of them is far greater than any church, or endorsed ecclesiastical dogma in which they changed, or eliminated the true name of God, thereby denigrating the very concept of God. Even Sir Isaac Newton wrote that the Anglican and Catholic churches, as well as, other churches did blasphemy in promoting the concept of the trinity, thereby violating the very First Commandment of God Yahweh. People have been deceived into believing Constantine's New Testament with the logos name of jesus christ. Many try to justify that name by saying it is Yeshua, or Yehoshua. Both of those names are Hebrew for Joshua son of Nun. (Neh. 8:17) In Hebrew Yahusha means Father, and Yahuah means Salvation. And the first three letters of those Hebrew words are "YAH" which is first three letters of YAHWEH, the one true God. The very First Commandment is "I Am Yahweh your God, who brought you out of the land of Egypt, out of the house of bondage, "You shall have no other gods before me." Det. 5:6-7

"Hear, Israel: Yahweh is our God. Yahweh is one. You shall love Yahweh your God with all your heart with all your soul, and with all your might." Det. 6:4

Even the tetragrammaton of YHWH is Yahweh. And **Yah** in Hebrew means **I AM**, which "AM" is the first two letters of the beginning of the name **AMEN**. The very opening of the Hebrew prayer, "**Amen Our Father who art in heaven, Holy is thy name.**" Even the doxology of the prayer is "**For thine is the kingdom, the power and all glory forever and ever Amen.**"

INDEX OF CHAPTERS

All excerpted passages from Old Testament books as contained in: World English Bible with Deuterocanonical/ Apocryphal & Hebrew Names Version updated version of American Standard Version Bible, copyrighted 1901 Philip Schaff translation, published by Thomas Nelson, N.Y. Public Domain

All excerpts from World English Bible including Catholic Deuterocannical all under umbrella of public domain.

if pages are all excerpts from Deuterocanical it will be listed at top of page, or verses deviate from World English Bible it will be noted by the verse

GLORIA OF MADONNA
April 25, 2007   Artist: Karen Sobek

CHAPTER ONE

TRUE LOVE

In order to understand the truth of biblical history you have to follow, not only, the people involved, but in conjunction of the timeline of the Prophets and Seers as contained in the Old Testament.

The New Testament Gospels were fragmented pieces of paper which did not contain the full text of information of the history of those books. During the reign of Constantine who wanted to form a Roman one world religion had Eusebeus write the contents of those Gospels based on a triad of gods from four pagan belief systems with a made up logos name from his sol invictus, the worship of the sun, and his son.

To understand the true Blessed Mother Mary, and her parents called Hannah and Elkanah, one must follow the people involved, and the time in which the events occurred. My book is a humble attempt to inform people of the truth of history, and the people involved, instead of following the convoluted, and forged history as contained in the New Testament Gospels. Even from the very beginning, the anti-god, didn't want people to learn the truth of the One True God, and made it a war of religion, a war against the light, a war against God Almighty Yahweh himself. This anti-god didn't want people to have the freedom to choose. They wanted to oppress and suppress the truth of the one true God, and true biblical history. The freedom to choose the one true God and have life, or choose death with the anti-god.

God Almighty Yahweh came to earth himself after seeing what evil had been doing to lead his flock astray with their perversions and worship of pagan idols.

Yahweh came to earth within the antiquities of Old Testament to save his children, his flock from their sins, to save their very souls simply out of love.

When on earth, he was born of Mary and known as Our Immanuel, who grew up to be the upright man, Yashar'El, a priest, our Savior which was prophesied by the prophets. He came to teach his people love, to adhere to the Covenant of God, and demonstrated the height of love for His flock by saving their very souls.

He came to earth out of love to save the good souls of his children, in that time of history. He was filled with such sorrow over the abominations that evil was doing to human beings, that this sorrow crushed, and pierced him emotionally that he gave his own life to save the very souls of those he loved.

Why do you think evil always attacks the good, the very children of God. Why do you think they always attack Jerusalem, the very footstool of God. It is out of hate for God, out of hate for the children of God, and wanted many to be condemned with them.

This evil, not only convoluted, but perverted the very facts of history, in which to deceive people into a continued worship of paganism through repetition of falsehoods.

God Yahweh came to earth in the beginning to save souls, and gave people the freedom to choose in order for you to save your own souls this time, and choose life. To get on your knees to confess your sins and beg for forgiveness, and follow His Commandments to have life.

To be in love with God is to be in communion with God. We are not here on earth by accident, we are here by God's design in which to help him in his battle against evil, to have truth known, so people can save their own souls. Evil wanted to do a pagan sacrifice, which is just another name for murder of the innocent. I don't believe in evil, nor do I believe in their paganism of sacrifice, for whom did you sacrifice, and to whom did you sacrifice too. What did you gain? Did you gain love, or did you gain hate. Did you help, or did you hinder. Whom did pagans sacrifice too, they sacrificed in name of their anti-god, to show their hatred for the one true God. Even the Romans, like the Nazi's did genocide practices, which is a mass murder of the innocent. This evil from the beginning acted with such hatred for God, and the very children of God. Even in the Book of Daniel, it says that after sixty-two weeks the anointed one will be slain. (Dan. 9:26) They wanted to eliminate the tree of life, eliminate and denigrate the name of God in their writings, and to pervert history so many would be deceived into participating in their pagan worship.

When a follower of the anti-god, Antiochus, was ruling he tried to bully a mother, and her seven sons into submission to evil, by breaking the very laws of the Covenant of God.

"Oh mother, that together with thy seven sons didst break the tyrant's force, and bring to nought his evil devices, and gavest an example of the nobleness of faith.

Thou wert nobly set as a roof upon thy sons as pillars, and the earthquake of the torments shook thee not at all. Rejoice therefore, pure-souled mother, having the hope of thy endurance certain at the hand of God. Not so majestic stand the moon amid the stars in Heaven as thou, having lit the path of thy seven star like sons unto righteousness, standest in honor with God; and thou art set in Heaven with them. For thy child-bearing was from the son of Abraham...Here lie an aged priest and a woman full of years and her seven sons through the violence of a tyrant desiring to destroy the Hebrew Nation.

They vindicated the rights of our people looking unto God and enduring the torments even unto death. And righteousness won the victory, and gave the crown to her athletes. Who but wondered at the athletes of the true law?...now these are the words that the mother of the seven sons, the righteous woman, spoke to her children: I was a pure maiden, and I strayed not from my father's house, and I kept guard over the rib that was build into Eve." (2nd Macc. 7:7-42 webc, Jer.15:5-9, 4th Book Maccabees Chapter 8)

Even from the beginning evil pagans wanted to destroy the Jewish nation, as they are trying today under the guise of religion, to eliminate the freedom of choice just out of hatred for God.

How many today are awake to the voice of the one true God? We are not here by accident, but by God's design. To be totally in love with God is to be in communion with God Yahweh. I was asked by heaven to write all the things that occurred in my life with God. Normally I would not do this for I am more reserved, and don't like to draw attention to myself, and how much I am in love with God. But I will try to relate my experiences.

I grew up in a Catholic household, and went to Catholic grade school and high school. They would issue prayer books to children stamped with the Vatican seal of approval, and as I was reading it, I came across a very odd line which stated that the chosen children of God was Islam. I questioned the parish priest and he said, "oh its just probably a mistake." Even then I was leery of the Catholic church doctrine.

Believe this or not, but when I was a teenager God appeared to me and said, "I have come to Anoint you with oil, let it run down to your neck and to your collar, and for all that you have tried to do out of love for me you have gained Paradise."

At that time I didn't know what I did to gain such love from Almighty God. What a gift to gain Paradise, but to me my greatest gift is my Father God Almighty Yahweh.

In my teenage years we went on a school trip to a Grotto in Maryland. As a teenager you want to have fun with your friends, but during this visit I was in a field by myself and heard a woman's voice, "There are children throwing rocks at my statue, please go over there and have them stop." I walked there and actually batted away the rocks they were throwing at the Blessed Mother Mary's statue, and scared them into running away. Walking back across the field, now slightly dirty, there was a woman standing there dressed in a long dress with a veil, asking me to approach her. My thoughts at the time, "great, now a foreigner wants to ask me directions, and I am not even from here." But I reluctantly went to her and she said to me, "I saw what you did to stop those children from throwing rocks." To my surprise she spoke perfect English, and I became embarrassed at my previous thoughts.

All of a sudden out of no where a older woman appeared to the right of her. She said, "Ann go with her to show her the way to her friends." As we walked across the field to the edge of the trees, the first woman's voice called out to me, as if she was next to me and said, "Karen turn around." So I did and she lifted her hand and blessed me, and I felt that blessing upon my face. She said to me, "You have great love inside of you."

As I turned around the woman named Ann, who was beside me, was now back at the other woman's side. Again, my thoughts, "God that woman can move fast to get back there so quickly." Had I known at the time that it was the Blessed Mother Mary, and her mother called Ann, or Hannah, I would have put my arms around her and not let her go.

Even when I grew older in my home town, I heard God's voice again saying, "I need you to enter that building and listen to what you hear and see, then come out and tell me."

So I entered a building called Opus Dei and felt such evil, and heard them talking of things that had nothing to do with love of God. I went back outside, and relayed what I saw and heard, and God said to me, "Good you saw and heard what I did."

I said to Him, "Why didn't you tell me ahead of time that there was so much evil there." His response to me, "If I told you what to expect it would have prejudiced your thoughts to look for what I saw, now I can use you as the true witness for Final Judgment."

He also said to me, "Sometimes I will have you travel to bear witness for me, then at other times you will stay still, and evil being stupid will send them to you."

Over the years evil wanted me dead several times. I took a position in Baltimore as a Operations Manager, and I had just started it when I began to have nose bleeds. I heard God tell me to go to Baltimore County Hospital for a good doctor was on duty. So I went and he admitted me into the hospital. He knew it was a virus of some kind, but couldn't identify it, and after three days I decided to check myself out of the hospital. This same doctor came to my place of employment along with a man dressed in a hazmat suit. He gave me several pills to take all at once, and told me that it was a military virus called Anthrax. They sprayed the office where my desk was, and gave me a regiment of pills to take for several days. If it wasn't for God, and this doctor I would have been murdered by this evil cabal.

Still at this job I heard the Trumpet of God sound, and the Gulf War broke out when Israel was attacked with Scud missiles from Iraq. After this occurred, I heard God again tell me to go into Washington, D.C to apply for a position in the printing office. So I went there and was sitting in there waiting for someone to come into the reception area. While there a man came into the reception area, and he looked like a Muslim. One of the male employees, came into the area, and didn't see me sitting in the corner, and addressed this man. This Mideastern Muslim immediately said to him, "I was sent here to get airplane manuals from you to learn to fly a commercial plane." The printing office man never asked him who he was, who sent him, or for any identification, but seemed to know that he had to give him the manuals, as if they were in a secret society.

After this I moved back into Pennsylvania, and after several years of moving again, I wound up in the middle of the state in Gettysburg. About this time the attack on America happened with the mass murder of people on 9/11/01. When it was reported that authorities couldn't understand how the Muslims got hold of airplane manuals which they found to fly the planes, I began to realize. I realized why God had sent me into D.C., and who I bore witness too. I notified the FBI of all that I witnessed.

I was in a small rented house in Gettysburg, when the same printing office man, who I witnessed give the airplane manuals to the Muslim, came up from D.C., and bought the very property on which I was renting. Again they tried to murder me with virulent viruses, staph infection, and loss of breaks on my car. The virulent virus blinded me in my left eye, and yet through all this attack on me by evil, all cause I bore witness to them, God had continued to save my life for my purpose on earth was still not complete.

There were other people I witnessed in Pittsburgh who were murdered, and I gave the police in Pittsburgh information on who I witnessed. These evil people have murdered entire families, including the murder of three woman. One of the woman was a close friend of mine, and one was even a Nun. It broke my heart for I tried to save them. My friend from Pittsburgh was actually in this area when she was murdered, and her body placed in a creek. I heard God's voice tell me to "stand still for if he sees you he will come after you, and I need you to do things for me yet." By the time I reached her she was already gone. I pulled her out of the creek, and kissed her hand while crying.

The Nun who was also from Pittsburgh was on a school trip to this area, when she was abducted, and I yelled for the police. I actually followed the car from here to Pittsburgh. They buried her in an old cemetery with a straw coming out of the ground. I dug with my bare hands to try to save her until the grounds keeper arrived. We both dug, but I couldn't save her in time. Even still to this day I have never gotten over the cruelty done to these woman, and I want justice upheld for them, and the lives of other people they murdered. These evil people extend from Pittsburgh to Maryland, and including this area which are in league with this luciferian cabal.

Even when I was in my early 20's I have always come to the defense of others. Even when a nursing assistant was ready to punch an elderly lady all cause she couldn't remember how to to sit down, I ran to stop the punch from hitting her. I yelled for security, and human resources to come and see me. They escorted the assistant out of the hospital, and I asked the human resource woman if this lady had any family. She said, "no." I told her "do you have paperwork that I could become her family," and she said "yes". So I signed the paperwork, and asked for every doctor to see me. They had her on so much medication that she could barely function. I was informed that she had a bad heart, and that she needed to remain on this one medication. Over the next several months I checked on her, and she was a functioning happy person. She died not long after this, and the hospital informed me that they would bury her in potters field. I said no for I would pay for her casket, and for her to be buried in the regular cemetery.

You have good people in every government, and even in every family. There are good people in the FBI not everyone is a rogue element within the agency.

In the course of these years one FBI agent got shot in defense of me, and I went to Bethesda Hospital to see him. He was not awake, but I laid my hand on his heart, and I talked to him. I told him how much I cared for him, but that he shouldn't have put himself in such danger for me, and I thanked him for his help in coming to the defense of me.

When I left the room, a FBI agent was standing guard at the door, and he had tears in his eyes. He said to me, "So many people would never thank us for putting our lives on the line in defense of this nation.," I thanked him for all he does.

I knew there were some rogue elements, but I didn't know how pervasive they were when I sent information to them. It is the same deep state, cabal that our President Trump is fighting within the government, the enemy, not just within government, but within America.

In all my past writings I had stated that I will not let the truth die with me, and so I keep fighting for my work is not completed for God Almighty. I wrote this so all would know the truth of what is really going on within this country.

I still didn't know even when I grew older what I would do to gain Paradise. So in my my middle years, after traveling to different places, my brother David came for a visit and asked me, "Why does God want us to love him, why doesn't he just command us too." I said to him, "David you have children, do you want to command them to love you, or do you want them to love you freely for who you are." He said, "No, I want them to love me for who I am." My response, "Well so does God, he gave you the freedom of choice, and he wants you to love him for who he is."

There has been other stories, but now that I am retired, I finally have the time to further my writings on my love of the one true God Yahweh. I wanted everyone to love him just like I do, but for centuries people have been indoctrinated into the Vatican deception and lies. Constantine had Eusebeus forge Gospels which perverted history with a belief in a mythical logos name of Iesus, a anti-god, which was based on pagan belief systems to form his one world Roman religion.

Then I heard God again, at this time in my life saying, "If you do write many people will come to hate you because of what you write. For they were led astray, and will hate you because of me." I said, "Evil hates me anyway, what's the difference. What matters to me is that everyone know who the One True God is Yahweh." I was informed that a miracle would take place. This miracle, like a metamorphosis, would astound many, and that it would make people finally realize. So now I have my answer of what I did to gain Paradise.

By the Grace of God Almighty Yahweh he gave this last opportunity, this final reprieve, before Final Judgment, to have the truth known. By Him doing this was for people to have the knowledge of the truth, and to have the freedom to choose, without evil's interference, in a effort to save their own souls. He gave the Ten Commandments to follow, and even came to earth Himself to teach people to turn away from evil, and to follow Him. This time its up to all to show God Yahweh that you love him in order to save your own souls. For the next time He comes, the second time, will be for Final Judgment.

My love of God and the truth is far greater then hate. He wanted to inform people of the truth, so they would freely love the One True God Yahweh, in an effort to save their own souls. My love of God and letting people know the truth of His Holy Name Yahweh is of far greater importance then the hatred of evil.

I write not for my glory, but for the Glory of the One True God, the Great I AM Amen, Yahweh. The very First Commandment, "I AM Yahweh, your God...You shall have no other gods before me." (Det. 5:6-7)

"I AM Yahweh, and there is no one else. Besides me, there is no God." (Is. 45:5)

There are children of God here on earth who are awakened to who they are, why there here, and what they are to do for God. We stand up for love of God, and have the fidelity of love for the one true God Yahweh. God calls upon all who hear him in which to fight this evil out of love. God the Almighty Yahweh has never stopped in his love of the good, and responds out of the height of love for them. If one were to analyze love, and just call it an intellectual thought of love, then what of the emotions of love? Yes, everything starts with a thought, but does it end with just a thought of love? Or does the height of true love reach into the very soul of you, and move you to an all-encompassing love of God.

For if it were just a thought alone, then all would be a passing thought. For we as humans are not infallible. The body dies, the thought processes cease to be. Then what of love? Does it remain a passing thought that dies when the body dies? The answer is a definite no.

For if love were just a thought alone then why would all souls strive for heaven, and the love of God. God's love is all encompassing, and each person on earth should strive to have an all-encompassing, empirical love of him. Love starts with a mere thought, but it should develop emotionally, and reach into the very center of you to the height of one's soul.

When you can think a thought of love, and let the emotions of that love overwhelm you within, then one has the beginnings of an all-encompassing love. I say beginnings, because if you take all the aspects of an encompassing love, and add an innumerable amount to what you feel, then you have a better understanding of the all-encompassing love of God.

To love with the totality of love from the heart of one's soul is to be in communion with God. The fidelity of love is to truly love the one true God. Even the very First Commandment states, "I am Yahweh your God...." you shall have no other gods before me." (Det. 5:6)

"Hear, Israel: Yahweh is our God. Yahweh is one. You shall love Yahweh your God with all your heart, with all your soul, and with all your might." (Det. 6:4-5)

If one uses a different name other then the one true God, then it is empty words which has no meaning, for you are using a pagan mythical name as a substitution for the one true God Yahweh. These empty words have no sincerity of the thoughts, or feelings that one wants to express. It would be like pouring water into a hand with open fingers. The precious water, or words of God should be heard and embraced, as all would cup their hands, so not to loose even one drop, of the precious gift of life, of true love, of light, of God himself.

Even poets have searched for the right words in which to describe the very feelings of the height of love. Composers of music have searched for the right combination of notes in which to express their emotions of love. Each one in its own movement of emotion to touch another being in the emotions of that love. Words without the height, the sincerity, and the fidelity of true love are simply words. The notes of a musical composition are simply random notes played out of tune. But when you have true love, with all sincerity and fidelity of heart, mind and soul, you have true love that reaches to the height of true love. Words with the melody in perfection of love's harmony with each other. The intertwining of such poetic melodies is a radiant symphony, a love song of true love which emanates, and is the essence of true love and light, of the Supreme God Yahweh.

The Blessed Mother Mary is such a gentle being who loves God with all of her soul. When on earth with her son, the amount of sorrow she endured should have never happened. The evil wanted to destroy life, to destroy love, to destroy the very tree of life. And that sorrow she endured was from the cruelty of evil. The very tears she shed, which came upon her face was one tear too many. I would have wiped away her tears out of love for such a beautiful gentle being as her, for one tear was one tear too many.

She is the Elect of God. Even in the Book of Tobit it stated, **Within you, generations after generation shall proclaim** their joy, and the **name of her who is Elect** shall endure through the generations to come." (Tobit 13:11-12)

The **gates of Jerusalem shall be built of Sapphire and of Emerald...**" (Tobit 13:21)

She was elected and gave birth to Our Savior, Yashar'El, the Upright One, who is referred in the Book of Isaiah as Immanuel.

CHAPTER TWO

HISTORY

To understand the true history one needs to read the Old Testament. For within all the books of the Torah, the Old Testament, contains the information of the people involved in the greatest event in history, and the time period in which the greatest event occurred with the birth of Our Savior. God in his infinite wisdom gave us clues which are contained in each of the books of the prophets and seers.

There has been so much confusion over the parents of the true Blessed Mother Mary, and over which Zechariah was it at the time, and was he the son of Iddo of Berechiah, or another. My book will help to clarify the true history of everything through the people involved, and the time period in which they lived.

For even in different Apographa writings, "**Joy is of the Saints**! And who shall put it on, but they alone? **Grace is of the elect**! And who shall receive it except those who trust in it from the beginning. **Love is of the elect**. And who shall put it on except those who have possessed it from the beginning." (Ode of Solomon)

The true Blessed Mother Mary the daughter of Hannah and Elkanah gave birth to our Savior, our Immanuel. "Dos't thou see that I dwell in a house of cedar, and the ark of God is lodged within skins?...because the Lord is with thee." (2nd Sam. 7:2)

To understand the people, and the date perimeter, one must look at certain specific and prominent people involved. Hannah and Elkanah and their son Samuel, along with King David and his three sons Daniel, Absalom, and Solomon along with the prophets Isaiah, Zechariah, Elijah, Jeremiah, and Ezekiel. There are certain people who's **names are only singular to those individuals, meaning no other was called by those names in Old Testament. Those names are: Samuel, David, Daniel, Absalom, and Solomon.** These are the key figures which I will further expand in my writing to help with the understanding, and the full view of this history within antiquities.

For instance in the book of Isaiah is the Song of Immanuel. This Song in Isaiah is contained in antiquities and relates to that timeline, not to the common era. Zechariah, and Mary's mother Hannah, or Ann is from the line of Phenuel of Asher; Daniel, Absalom, Solomon of David, and the Maccabees all lived within antiquities.

Many Old Testament books contain pertinent information, such as Psalms, along with The Song of Solomon to the timeline, and lineage of Mary, and her parents Hannah and Elkanah.

The Song of Solomon, or known as the Song of Songs.

In Hebrew the spelling of **Hannah is Shoshanna meaning Lily, or Rose, and is also spelled Channah meaning Grace, as in the Spirit of Grace, or the children of Grace.**

"I am the rose of Sharon, the **lily of the valleys**. - As a lily among the thistles, so is my love among maidens. - As an apple tree among the trees of the orchard, so is my Beloved among the young men." The Song of Songs 2:1-3 **Chava in Hebrew means Eve the mother of all.** (Gen. 3:20)

Mary and Mariah are a variants of Miriam and Martha which are the two daughters of the Lily, Grace called Hannah. Mariah is a Hebrew name which is a variant of Moriah the Temple Mount, and its meaning means The Lady, or Teacher.

In the New Testament Martha is a variant of Marta a Roman name.

The reference to thistles is referring to Lebanon. "Your cheeks, behind your veil, are halves of pomegranate. There are sixty queens and eighty concubines (and countless maidens). But my dove is unique, mine unique and perfect. She is the **darling of her mother**, the favorite of the one who bore her. The maidens saw her, and **proclaimed her blessed."**

(The Song of Songs 6: 6-8) The reference to half's of a pomegranate could be in reference to twin daughters of which in New Testament books refers to the other Mary, the Lady.

Hannah is Channah, also called Anna or Ann, and Elkanah was the husband of Hannah. (1st Samuel 1:1-2) In the Book of Samuel, (1st Sam 2:21), **"Yahweh visited Hannah; she conceived and gave birth to three sons and two daughters."** I believe the children were: **Samuel, Abijah, Eliezar (Greek - Lazarus), Mariah & Miriam with a variant in English Martha and Mary, Samuel, Abijah, Eliezar the sons of Elkanah and Hannah.** (1st Chrn. 6:8-15) The name of the son Eliezar, and daughters are contained within scripture, and through their lineage which lived in the antiquities of Old Testament.

The Blessed Mother Mary, contrary to belief was not of lowly birth, but of Royalty of the line of King David. I have done several oil paintings of the Queen of Heaven, but not even my humble attempt to paint her beautiful face can compare to the beauty of her soul. Not even an actual photograph can compare to her beauty. She like God Yahweh are are un-compared in their radiant beauty. As each snowflake has its own unique beauty, they may look the same at first glance, and they are of the same, but each has its own beauty. For as they originate in the Heavens from one place, each snowflake has its own beauty, but are still all of the whole. Even such renowned artists as Michael Angelo, their paint and brush could not have formed a line of blue more beautiful. Not even sculptures by Roden could have molded such perfection of beauty that is so un-compared, for the artist is but one, the Creator of All souls, who was and who is the Great I AM, Yahweh. And in the Hebrew transliteration of the name, YAH, the first three letters of his name, means I AM, and in the first two letters of Amen is, AM, as in I AM.

Even in the Book of Ezekiel it says that all souls belong to God Almighty Yahweh, "All souls are mine." (Ezk. 18:4) Even throughout Old Testament God had declared who he was, "I myself am Yahweh. Besides me, there is no Savior." (Is. 43:11) And that everyone would come to know his real name in that day. (Is. 52:6) For God Almighty is our hope, our salvation, our very fountain of life. (Joel 3:16, 18)

"Blessed be Yahweh, the God of Israel, from everlasting even to everlasting. All the people said, "Amen," and praised Yahweh." (1st Chrn. 16:36)

Within the New Testament books there is some accurate information, however, they were excerpts from Old Testament books to justify and add credence to Constantine's logos myths, and timeline of events. For instance in the Book of Luke it stated that Zechariah belonged to the Abijah section of priesthood, with Elizabeth being descendant of Aaron. In the Book of Zechariah (1:1) **Zechariah the son of Berechiah, the son of Iddo, the prophet.** Abijah and Samuel were also the sons of Elkanah and Hannah. (1st Chrn. 6:8-15)

Samuel's sons are Joel and Abijah. (1st Sam. 8:1-2) Zechariah is a brother of Elkanah, and was uncle to Mary and the rest of her siblings.

Elizabeth in Hebrew is Elisheba, and she was the wife of Aaron. (Ex. 6:23) Elisheba is also the daughter of Amminadab, and sister of Nahshon. Amminadab time of David. (1st Chrn. 15:11)

In the book of Luke (Luke 1:5-7) it states that Zechariah's wife was Elizabeth daughter of Aaron. I have found no reference in Old Testament to the name of Zechariah's wife.

Simeon who is mentioned in (Luke 2:25-27) was told by the Holy Spirit that he would not see death until he had set eyes on the Lord. Simeon is the second son of Leah and Jacob. (also ref. Ist Macc. 2:1-7) **Sons of Simeon: Shaul, his son Shallum and Zaccur his son Shimei.** (1st Chrn. 4:24-27) Shimeon is one of the sons of Harim. (Ezra 10:31)

Mary's mother Anna or Ann, Hannah was the daughter of Phanuel, of Perez of the tribe of Asher. **Hannah's mother was Serah**, the sister of Immah, Ishvah, Ishvi, **Beriah.** (1st Chrn. 7:30)

In Hebrew the spellings of Phanuel is also written as **Penuel meaning the face of God.** "The **sons of Judah: Perez, Hezron, Carmi, Hur, Shobal**" (1st Chrn. 4:1)

"These are the sons of the father Etam, **Jazreel, Ishma and Idbash. The name of their sister was Hazzelelponi. Penuel became father of Gedor, and Ezer father of Hushah. These are the sons of Hur, the first-born of Ephrathah, the father of Bethlehem.**" (1st Chrn. 4:3-4) (see references Dan. 13:1-3, Det. 33:1-29 and Judith 15:8)

So in the Book of Luke the prophecy of Simeon and Anna are accurate, but not in the timeline of New Testament books.

Uzziah was the son of Micah of the tribe of Simeon. (Judith 6:15)

According to the book of Luke, Zechariah's son John roamed the wilderness, "...through the whole Jordan district proclaiming a baptism of repentance for the forgiveness of sins, as it is written in the book of the sayings of the prophet Isaiah: "A voice cries in the wilderness: prepare a way for the Lord, make his paths straight." (Luke 3:3-4)

The following passages were excerpt from Isaiah, "the path of the upright man is straight, you smooth the way of the upright." (Is. 26:7) Again this was done to add credence to book of Luke.

Elijah was referenced to being John the son of Zechariah. "A voice of one who cries out, "**Prepare the way for Yahweh in the wilderness!**. Make a level highway in the desert for our God." (Is. 40:3) Elijah was one of the sons of Jeroham as well as Elkanah, and Zechariah.

The **upright one is Yashar'El, Yahweh our Savior who came to earth and was born in antiquities in the month and day** of **September 25th, the first day of Autumn, Feast of Tabernacles.** The references to Yashar is contained within the Books of Joshua and Samuel, which refers to the Book of the Just.

When **Solomon asked God** if he would keep his **promise made to David and live among men** is also a corroboration to the timeline of history. Another verification to the dates of history is to the name of **Immanuel and Yashar'El**, as contained in the Books of Deuteronomy and Isaiah.

"Now therefore, **God of Israel**, please **let your word be verified, which you spoke to your servant David my father. But will God in very deed dwell on the earth.**" (1st Kgs.8:26-27)

Even in the Book of **Isaiah**, who lived and died within the 8th century, and was one of the prophets of Yahweh. He was the son of Amoz and lived during the time of **Uzziah, Jotham, Ahaz and Hezekiah.** Within the Book of Isaiah is also the sign of the **Immanuel** which in Hebrew means "**with us is God.**" (Is. 7:10-14)

The Hebrew Transliteration of **Immanuel** is:
IM = I Am IMMANU GOD WITH US
MAN = MAN CREATION
U = TENT PEG
EL = GOD

"I drive him like a **peg** into a firm place; he will become a throne of glory for his father's house." (Is. 22:23) Or in Zechariah "From him will come **cornerstone** and from him the (nail) **tent peg**." (Zech. 10:4 also Judges 5:26)

The prophecy of the Messiah's birth wasn't for hundreds of years latter, but within Isaiah's life. "For there is a **child born for us,** a son given to us and dominion is laid on his shoulders. His **name will be called** Wonderful, Counselor, **Mighty God, Everlasting Father,** Prince of Peace." (Is. 9:5-6) Just this passage alone shows the present tense by saying a child is born to us, not a future event. The time perimeter and lineage is also confirmed with "A shoot will come out of the **stock of Jesse**, a branch out of his **roots will bear fruit. Yahweh's Spirit will rest** on him: the **spirit of wisdom and understanding, the** spirit of counsel and might, the spirit of knowledge and the fear of Yahweh. (The fear of **Yahweh is his breath.**) (Is. 11:1-2)

The reference to branch **of Jesse is with line of David**, and that God **Yahweh came to earth** to fulfill his promise that he made that He would **live among men – Yahweh is his breath.**

The path (way) of the **upright man is straight**, you smooth the way of the upright. "Yes, in the way of the just is uprightness. You who are upright make the path of the righteous level. Yes, in the way of your judgments, Yahweh, we have waited for you. Your name and your renown are the desire of our soul." (Is. 26:7-8)

By saying **upright man is straight** is in reference to **Yashar'El** as referenced also in the books of Samuel with the **Book of the Just** (2nd Samuel 1:18, and in Joshua 13:2), as well as, the name of **Jeshurun** also spelled in Hebrew Cepheras as **Yasharun**. (Det. 33:26 and Is. 44:1-8) Hebrew Cepher states also that **the name** means, "**I Am He who breathes life**".

The Hebrew transliteration of the name is as follows:

YAH = I AM, I AM AMEN
SHA = SAVES
RESH = THE FIRST/CHOSEN ONE
EL = GOD
NUN = SEED/KINGSHIP

"...THERE WAS A KING IN JESHURUN.." DET. 33:5

The Messiah's birth wasn't at the turn of the century as Constantine wanted everyone to believe in his rewrite of history, but actually occurred in antiquities as stated in the Book of Isaiah. Even in the Book of **Zechariah** who was a prophet, and the son of **Berechiah, son of Iddo**, stated that **Yahweh** had said, "For I, says Yahweh, will be to her a wall of life around it, and I will be the glory in the middle of her." (Zech. 2:4-5, 10)

Within the Book of Isaiah is the **Song of Immanuel. "Behold, the virgin will conceive, and bear a son, and shall call his name Immanuel." (Is. 7:14)**

I will set your stones in beautiful colors, and lay your **foundations on Sapphires..**" (Is. 54:13) "Arise, shine, for your **light has come, and Yahweh's glory** has risen on you..... Yahweh will arise on you, and his glory shall be seen on you. Nations come to your light, and kings to the brightness of your rising." (Is. 60:1-3)

Even in the Book of Tobit, "A bright light shall shine over all the regions of the earth; many nations shall come from far away, from all the ends of the earth, to dwell close to the Holy name of the Lord God with gifts in their hands for the King of Heaven. **Within you, generations after generation shall proclaim** their joy, and the **name of her who is Elect** shall endure through the generations to come." (Tobit 13:11-12)

The **gates of Jerusalem shall be built of Sapphire and of Emerald...**" (Tobit 13:21)

Tobit also stated that he was glad that one of line of his family was so Bless through Tobiel his father, son of **Hananiel**, son of Aduel, son of Abael, son of Raphael, son of Raguel, of **Asiel** of the tribe of Naphtali. (Tobit 1:1)

Berechiah and Elkanah were gatekeepers to the Ark. (1ˢᵗ Chrn. 15:23) The priests were Shebaniah, Joshaphat, Nethanel, Amasai, **Zechariah....**(1ˢᵗ Chrn. 15:24)

"Of the Levites: **Shemaiah** son of Hasshub, son of Azrikam, son of Hashabiah of the **sons of Merari; and** Bakbakkar, Heresh, Galal, **Mattaniah the son of Mica,** son of **Zichri,** son of **Asaph,** and **Obadiah** son of **Shemaiah,** son of Galal, son of Jeduthun, and **Berechiah son of Asa, son of Elkanah..**" (1ˢᵗ Chrn. 9:14-16)

"**Sons of Solomon: Rehoboam, Abijah his son, Asa his son, Jehosphaphat his son, Joram..Ahaziah..Joash... Amaziah...Azariah..Jotham...Ahaz...Hezekiah...Manasseh..Amon..Josiah his son.**" (1ˢᵗ Chrn. 3:10-15)

In the **days of Joiakim** the heads of the priestly families were: family of **Seraiah,** Meraiah, Jeremiah, Hananiah; of Ezra, Meshullam; of Amariah... **Joseph;** of Harim, Adna; of Meraioth, Helkai; of **Iddo, Zechariah....Joiarib.**" (Neh. 12:12-16) **Seraiah** was the scribe in **King David's** administration. (2ⁿᵈ Sam. 8:18)

"These lived in the **days of Joiakim son of Jeshua, son of Jozadak, and in the days of Nehemiah** the governor, and of **Ezra,** priest and scribe." (Neh. 12:26)

Heads of the families who set out in the reign of Artaxerxes from Babylon, "Of the sons of Phinehas: Gershom; of the sons of Ithamar: **Daniel; of the sons of David..**" (Ezra 8:1-2)

In the Book of Daniel (13: 1-3) it mentions that in Babylon lived a man called **Joakim who married Susanna daughter of Hilkiah, daughter of Judah, however, this was not the father and mother of the Blessed Mother Mary.**

Susanna daughter of Hilkiah and her husband Joakim were of the line of Zadok of Levi.

"After these events in the reign of Artaxerxes king of Persia, **Ezra son of Seraiah,** son of **Azariah,** son of **Hilkiah,..**" (Ezra 7:1-2)

In the Book of Judith, **Joakim** was high priest residing in Jerusalem, which is **not the father of Mary** as stated in the Gospels of the New Testament. (Judith 4:5 and Daniel 13:1)

Within the New Testament books there are some factual information.

"**There was one Anna, a prophetess, the daughter of Phanuel, of the tribe of Asher (she was of a great age, having lived with a husband seven years from her virginity, and she had been a widow for about eighty-four years**), who didn't depart from the temple, worshiping with fasting and petitions night and day." (Luke 2:36-38)

"...**Simeon blessed** them, and said to Mary, his mother, "Behold, this child is set for the falling and the rising of many in Israel, and for a sign which is spoken against." (Luke 2:34)

Hannah wasn't a widow for eight-four years, for when her own son Samuel died during the time of David, she was about 69 years of age. Her husband Elkanah died during the invasion of Aramaeans in the time of David, and many were carried away captive. This is when Daniel was probably deported. (2ⁿᵈ Chrn. 28:7-8)

Hannah was also known as a prophetess.

In Bethulia the chief men were **Uzziah son of Mica of the tribe of Simeon.** (Judith 6:15) **Judith** was the **daughter of Merari son of Ox, of Joseph, of Oziel, of Elkiah, of Ananias son of Gideon, son of Raphaim, of Ahitub of Elijah, of Hilkiah.** (Judith 8:1)

During the water shortage where Judith heard of what **Uzziah** had said went to talk to the elders in Bethulia. (Judith 8:9-11)

"Before Zerubbabel be a plain! He will pull out the keystone..." (Zech. 4:7) "See now, your king comes to you; he is righteous, and having salvation; lowly, and riding on a donkey, even on a colt, the foal of a donkey." (Zech. 9:9) To confirm also what was stated by Solomon about God living among men was "...the **House of David will be like God** (like the angel of Yahweh) at their head." (Zech. 12:8)

"....in the **days of Uzziah King of Judah. Yahweh my God will come....**" (Zech. 14:5)

"And Yahweh will be king over all the earth. In that day, **Yahweh will be one, and his name one.**" (his name unique.) (Zech. 14:9-10)

Zechariah was of great age, but according to New Testament, his son was John.

Zachariah is of the division of Abijah (who is is the son of Samuel of Elkanah).

Adaiah son of Jeroham, son of Peleliah son of Amzi, son of Zechariah, son of Pashur, son of Malchijah." (Neh. 11:12) Elijah was a brother of Zechariah of the sons of Jeroham.

Mary who was to give birth to the Messiah, Immanuel, the upright one called Yashar'El. "..Jeshurun whom I have chosen." (Is. 44:2) "One man will say, 'I am Yahweh's,' and another will be called by name of Jacob, and another will write with his hand 'to Yahweh,' and be surnamed Israel." (Is. 44:5 see also Jeshurun Det. 33:26)

CHAPTER THREE

LINEAGE

So Immanuel means God is with us, and Yashar'El means I Am one who saves, the first chosen one called Yahweh.

Our Messiah was born in antiquities, and in the Book of Psalms, "**Yahweh says to my Lord, "Sit at my right hand and I will make your enemies a footstool for your feet**." (Ps. 110:1)

So in this Psalm the Lord sits at the right hand of King David. "Light dawns in the darkness for the upright, gracious, merciful, and righteous." (Ps. 112:4) "I am Yahweh, and there is no one else. Besides me, there is no God.' (Is. 45:5)

Truly, **God is hidden with you, the God of Israel, the Savior**. (Is. 45:15, 2nd Chrn. 6:18)

Within the New Testament books there are accurate excerpts, however, these passages are drawn from Old Testament books to justify and add credence to Constantine's logos theories and timeline of events. For instance in the Book of Luke it stated that Zechariah belonged to the Abijah section of priesthood, with Elizabeth being descendant of Aaron, is taken from the Book of Zechariah (1:5-8). Abijah and Samuel were also the son of Elkanah and Hannah. (1st Chrn. 6:8-15) Samuel's sons are Joel and Abijah. (1st Sam. 8:1-2) Simeon who is mentioned in (Luke 2:25-27) and was told by Holy Spirit that he would not see death until he had set eyes on the Lord. Simeon is the second son of Leah and Jacob. (Ist Macc. 2:1-7 webc) However there was another Shimeon during that time. (see lineage chart next page)

Mary's mother Anna or Hannah was the daughter of Phanuel of the tribe of Asher. **Hannah's mother was Serah**, the sister of Immah, Ishvah, Ishvi, **Beriah.** (1st Chrn. 7:30)

In Hebrew the spellings of Phanuel is also written as **Penuel meaning the face of God**. "The **sons of Judah: Perez, Hezron, Carmi, Hur, Shobal**" (1st Chrn. 4:1)

Of the sons of Etam, **Jazreel, Ishma and Idbash**, whose **sister** was called **Hazzelelponi. Penuel** became father of Gedor, Ezer father of Hushah. These are the sons of **Hur, the first-born of Ephrathah, father of Bethlehem.** (1st Chrn. 4:3-4)

(Dan. 13:1-3, 2nd Sam. 2:18-21, Det. 33:1-29 and Judith 15:8)

Sons of Asaph: Zechariah and Mattaniah. (2nd Chrn. 29:13) **Jonathan (John) was the son of Uzziah.** (1st Chrn. 27:25) also Jonathan was David's uncle. (1st Chrn. 27:32)

So in the Book of Luke the prophecy of Simeon and Anna are accurate, but not in the timeline of New Testament books which were forged by Constantine to the Roman empire.

Chart Lineage Time period is 924BCE-794BCE

Simeon:

Shaul, Shallam, his son Mishma, Zaccur his son and **Shimei** son Ethan Micah his son Uzziah his son Johnathan

Levi:

Gershom, Merari, Kohath - his son Amram, Izhak, Uzziel son Micah, brother Isshiah son Zechariah and Hebron. **Brother of Micah, Isshiah.**
Kohath of Izhar and brother of Kohath son is Korah, Zichri
Harim son Malchijah father of Pashur who's son is **Zechariah**
sons of Harim Masseiah and Elijah and Shemaiah, **Shimeon, Shemiah son of Nethanel, Obadiah son of Shemaiah. Buzi father of Ezekiel,** and **Delaiah of Levi**

Gershom:

Libni and Shemei. Of **Libni: Joah, Iddo son is Asaph son Abinadah, son Eleazar. Iddo son Ahinadab** of Shemei – his son Uzzah, son Shimea of Merari.

Asher:

Michael his son **Shimea,** son **Berechiah,** son **Asaph. Beriah, Hannah of Penuel, of Perez of Asher.******

Perez:

Hezron, son **of Korah,** of Ebiasaph of Assir of Tahath, of **Zephaniah,** of Azariah, of Joel of Elkanah, of Amassi of Mahith, of Elkanah, of Zuph

Benjamin:	Bela, Becher....
	Bela: Ezbon, Uzzi, Uzziel, Jerimoth. Uzzi son Izrahiah.
	Izrahiah sons: Michael, Obadiah, Joel, Isshiah.
	Becher: Zemirah, Joash, Elizer, Elioenai, Omri, Jeremoth, Abijah, Anathoth.
	Joash son Gideon

| Issachar: | Tola son Uzzi, son Izrahiah |

| Merari: | Berechiah son Shimea, of Michael of Sethur of Asher. Shemaiah son Obadiah |

| Kohath : | Amminadab, son Korah, son Assir, Elkanah, son Joel, son of Zephaniah of Korah |

| brother | Amminadab son of Assir, son Uriel, son Uzziah and sons to Toah, son Eliel, son Jeroham |

| Asaph | Jeroham sons are: Elijah, Asaph, Zichri, Adaiah, Elkanah, Heman, Zechariah (Azariah) |

| Hezron: | Ram, Amminadab, Nahshon, Salma, Boaz, Obed, Jesse. Sons of Jesse: Eliab, |
| ***** | Abinadab, Shimea, Nethanel, Ozem, David their sisters Zeruiah and Abigail. Zeruiah sons:Abishai, Joah... |

Gershom of Levi, Merari: Libni, Shemei

Michael	Iddo	Ethni				
Jahath	Zimmah	Harim sons:				
Shimei	Joah	Maaseiah,		Malchijah,	Elijah,	Shemaiah,
Zimmah	Iddo	sons		son		son
Ethan	Shimei	Zephaniah &	Neriah	Pashur		Obadiah
Adaiah	Uzzah		Baruch	Zechariah		

Zerah	Shimea		Amzi
Ethni	Haggiah		
Merari		Asaph	Of Zimmah
Shimei		Abinadab	Joah
Berechiah		Eleazar	Iddo
Asaph			Shimei

Chart Lineage Time period is 924BCE-794BCE

time of David of the Levites:

Nahor, Buzi son Ezekiel (Jehezkel), Delaiah Jehoiarib, Jedaiah, Malchijah, Mijamin, Jeshua

Of Heman:

Pedaiah sons: Zerubabble and Shimei, Parosh his sons Mijamin, son Eleazar Zerubbable sons: Meshullam, Hananiah son Zedekiah

Sons of Seraiah:

Asiel, Asaiah-Tobit-Tobias to Deborah

Malchijah

Asaiah

Baaseiah

Michael

Shimea

Berechiah-brother Ethan of Shimei

Sons of Jeroham:

time of David of the Levites:

Nahor, Buzi son Ezekiel (Jehezkel), Delaiah
Jehoiarib, Jedaiah, Malchijah, Mijamin, Jeshua

Of Herman:

Pedaiah sons: Zerubabble and Shimei, Parosh his sons Mijamin, son Eleazar
Zerubbable sons: Meshullam, Hananiah son Zedekiah

Sons of Seraiah:

Asiel, Asaiah-Tobit-Tobias to Deborah

Malchijah	Asaiah
Baaseiah	
Michael	
Shimea	
Berechiah-brother Ethan of Shimei	

Son of Jeroham:

Berechiah *******Asaph	Heman	Elkanah	Zichri	Adaiah	Zechariah (Azariah)	Elijah
sons	sons: Uzziel, Shebuel	children	son	son	son	
Mattithias, Zichri	Bukkiah, Mattaniah	Samuel, Abijah, Eliezar	Elishaphat	Haziah	Uzziah	
Joah, Zechariah	& Jerimoth	Mary & Mariah		Maaseiah	Athaiah	
*****Joseph, Zaccur		Samuel sons:		Jeremoth	Ahaziah	
Nethaniah		Joel & Abijah			Joiarib	
Zichri son Joel		Heman Asa			Jedaiah, Adaiah	
Joel son Mattaniah		Jehoshaphat			Mattathias	
			Azariah		John	

Nathan (of David) Amaziah Zechariah's son: Amariah
               Uzziah

Azariah   Azariah

       Beeri   Uzziah (Azariah) Ahitub------------ Ahitub

       Hoshea Seraiah, Jonathan,   Zadok
              Jotham

   Nahum   Asiel, Ahaz
           Asaiah

   Amos   Tobit Hezekiah   sons
   Mattithias   Azariah, Shallum
                   Hilkiah-sons: Amaziah
                    & Jeremiah

              Amaziah of Hilkiah

      Amoz brother of ---

       Isaiah   Hezekiah
                 Manasseh, Amariah
                   Cushi
                  Zephaniah

         Jonah son of Amittai

The following people were in the time of King David 877BCE-837BCE.
From Solomon and his sons from 838BCE-623BCE Some of the people in Jerusalem were:
King David's brothers Shimea and Elihu
Of David and his daughters and sons which includes Absalom, Daniel.
Asiel father of Tobit and his son Tobias
Gershoms' son Shebuel of Moses his brother Eliezer, Rehabiah his son, Jeshaiah, Joram his son and Zichri, and his son Shelomoth.

Amminadab, son Korah, son Assir; Elkanah, son Joel, son of Zephaniah of Korah. Amminadab son of Assir, son Uriel, son Uzziah and sons to Toah, son Eliel, son Jeroham who's sons are: Elijah, Asaph, Zichri, Adaiah, Elkanah, Heman, Zechariah. Son of Zichri is Mica. Asa son of Berechiah of Iddo of Elkanah. Becher, Bela his son Uzziel

The Prophets and Seers:

Daniel, son of David. **Samuel** son of Hannah and Elkanah. **Nathan** of David **Micah** son of Uzziel. **Jeremiah** son of Hilkiah. **Isaiah** son of Amoz. **Ezekiel** son of Buzzi. **Iddo, Zechariah son of Berechiah the son of Iddo. Hoshea** son of Beeri. **Obadiah** son of Shemaiah of Zerubbabel. Haggai **son of Shealtiel.**

Elijah son of Zichri of Jeroham. **Elisha. Obed** son of Azariah. **Asaph** of Berechiah of **Iddo. Amos** son of Nahum. **Malachi** brother of Nathaniel and Josiah. **Zephaniah** son of Heman. **Habakkuk** son of Shioua Lovit. **Nahum** father of **Amos. Joel** son of Pethuel. **Jonah** son of Amittai.

Elkanah of Jeroham, and Hannah children: **Samuel, Abijah, Eliezar, Mary and Mariah. Korah his son Assir, Elkanah. Of Samuel: Joel and Abijah. Heman of Joel, and Asa of Abijah of Samuel. Jehoshaphat of Asa.**
Adaiah son of Jeroham, of Pelaliah, of Amzi, of **Zechariah**, of **Pashur** son of **Malchijah. Adaiah son of Joiarib, son of Zechariah. Baruch, son of Colhozeh, son of Haydah, son of Adaiah, son of Joiarib, son of Zechariah of Shilonites.**
Josiah and **Asaiah.** of Levi: Nahor, Buzi son Ezekiel (**Jehezkel**), Delaiah, Jehoiarib, Jedaiah, **Malchijah, Mijamin, Jeshua**
Asaph son of Berechiah of Iddo his sons are: Zaccur, **Joseph**, Nethaniah. Of **Jeduthun** his son Gedliah, Zeri, Jeshuah, **Shimei**, Hashabiah, **Mattithiah, Zechariah. Uzziah** his son Shaul.
Mattathias, son of John, son of Simeon, son of Joiarib his son Jedaiah, of the sons of Perez. Mattathias is father of Maacabees.

Heman son of Joel of Samuel. Heman's sons: **Bukkiah, Nataniah, Uzziel**, Shebuel, **Jerimoth** Hananiah, Hanani, **Mattaniah**, Masseiah, Obed-Edom.

Sons **of Harim** – Maaseiah, **Elijah, Shemaiah, Shimeon**
Mattithiah son of Shallum. Uzziah, Azariah son Seraiah, Jonathan, and Amaziah. Issachar son is **Omri of Michael.**
Ishmaeah son of **Obadiah**. Mica. **Zadok sons Shallum**, Ahimazz and his son **Jonathan.**

To understand the lineage of people and their correspondence to the timeline of history, it is important to read excerpts of those people as contained in Holy Scripture. Specifically to such people as Zechariah, Mattathias, and their relationship to Mary.

Sons of Simeon: Shaul his son Shallum..Zaccur his son Shimei. (1ˢᵗ Chrn. 4:24-27)
Son of Shimei is Mattathias, the son of John, son of Simeon, son of Joiarib. (Neh. 11:10, 1ˢᵗ Chrn. 25:3)
Uzziah his son Shaul. (1ˢᵗ Chrn. 6:6-10) **Korah son Assir, Elkanah..Assir** (1ˢᵗ Macc. 3)
Absalom and **Mattithias is mentioned in Book of Maccabees as the father of Maccabees. Mattithias is also Mattathiah** (Neh. 8:4, 1ˢᵗ Chrn. 15:18, 21) referenced as Clopas husband of Martha in New Testament in (Luke 10) and (John 19:25)

The **sons of Asaph, Zechariah and Mattaniah and of the sons of Heman, Jehuel and Shimei** and of the sons of Jeduthun, **Shemaiah and Uzziel to cleanse Yahweh's house.******
(2ⁿᵈ Chrn. 29:12-14) Jeshua became the father of Joiakim, he became father of Eliashib...his son Joiada...**Joiada the father of Jonathan** and his son Jaddua. (Neh. 12:1-11)

Children of Judah, Athaiah, son of Uzziah, son of Zechariah, son of Amariah, son of Shephatiah, son of Maholalel children of Perez. The son of **Baruch son of Colhozeh**, son of Hazaiah, son of **Adaiah, son of Joiarib, son of Zechariah, son of the Shilonites. All sons of Perez who lived in Jerusalem. Jedaiah, son of Joiarib.** Amaziah, Azariah sons of Hilkiah. Azariah father of Seraiah. Ahitub father of Zadok of Levi. (Neh. 11:3-7, 1ˢᵗ Chrn. 6:11-45)
The upright one is Yashar'El, **Yahweh our Savior** who came to earth and was born in antiquities in the month and day of **September 25ᵗʰ, the first day of Autumn, Feast of Tabernacles.**

"I will set your stones in beautiful colors, and lay your foundations with Sapphires.." (Is. 54:13)
"Arise, shine; for your **light has come, and Yahweh's glory has risen** on you..

The nations come to your light, and kings to the brightness of your rising. (Is. 60:1-3)

Even in the Book of Tobit, "A bright light shall shine over all the regions of the earth; many nations shall come from far away, from all the ends of the earth, to dwell close to the Holy name of the Lord God with gifts in their hands for the King of Heaven. Within you, generations after generation shall proclaim their joy, and the **name of her who is Elect** shall endure through the generations to come." (Tobit 13:11-12)

The gates of Jerusalem shall be built of Sapphire and of Emerald..." (Tobit 13:21)

Tobit was a descendant of Asaiah of Asiel of Seraiah of Naphtali, and some scholars state that the Book of Tobit was written during the dispersion around 4-5th century. In my chart it puts it at the time of Uzziah and Zechariah in the **8th century of 879-782 BCE.**

Berechiah and Elkanah were doorkeepers to the Ark. (1st Chrn. 15:23) The priests were Shebaniah, Joshaphat, Nethanel, Amasai, **Zechariah, Banaiah, Eliezer.** (1st Chrn. 15:24)

"Of the Levites: **Shemaiah** son of Hasshub, son of Azrikam, son of Hashabiah of the **sons of Merari;** Bakbakkar, Heresh, Galal, **Mattaniah son of Mica,** son of **Zichri,** son of **Asaph, Obadiah** son **of Shemaiah,** son of Galal, son of Jeduthun, and **Berechiah son of Asa, son of Elkanah.."** (1st Chrn. 9:14-16)

"The history of King David, from first to last, is this not recorded in the **Annals of Samuel the Seer,** the **Annals of Nathan the Prophet,** and **Annals of Gad the Seer....**" (1st Chrn. 29:29-30)

When **David was in Hebron he had six children born to him,** one of which was **Daniel** by his wife Abigail of Carmel. The second was **Absalom son of Maacah** the daughter of Talmai King of Geshur with the fourth being Adonijah son of Haggith. (1st Chrn. 3:1-4)

Elijah the Tishbite was during the time of Ahab who he made to repent. **Ahab was king of Samaria and Jehoshaphat, son of Asa, was king of Israel. Elijah, of Hilkiah, of Judith, and Berechiah, son of Asa, of Elkanah.** (1st Kngs. 22:41, 1st Chrn. 9:15, and Judith 8:1) **Elijah was also the son of Jeroham.** (1st Chrn. 8:26-27) as well as, **Elkanah being the son of Jeroham.**

The **foundations of the Temple of Yahweh was begun by Solomon** and it took seven years to complete. "**Look, I am going to send my messenger to prepare a way before me. And the Lord you are seeking will suddenly enter his Temple....**" (Malachi 3:1, Is. 40:3)

In Hebrew the meaning of the **name of Elijah** has its origin in **Eliyyahu meaning "my God is Yahweh."**

Isaiah the prophet was also in time of **Azariah son of Amaziah**. (2nd Kgs. 15:1-8)
Hezekiah son of Ahaz, and his mother's name was Abi the daughter of Zechariah.
(2nd Kngs 18:1-3) All these people were in the timeline of David, and Solomon.
"Sons of Kohath: Amram, Izhar, Hebron, Uzziel: four in all. Sons of Amram: Aaron and Moses."
(1st Chrn. 23:12-13)
"Sons of Moses: Gershom and Eliezer." (1st Chrn. 23:15)
"Sons of Uzziel: Micah first, Isshiah second." (1st Chrn. 23:20)
Sons of Kohath: **Heman was the grandson of Samuel and son of Joel of Samuel.** (1st Chrn. 6:33)
"The Levites then appointed **Heman son of Joel, Asaph son of Berechiah, one of his brothers Ethan...**" (1st Chrn. 15:17)

OUR LADY
December 26, 2008 Artist: Karen Sobek

Sons of Israel: Reuben, Simeon, Levi, Judah, Issachar, Zebulon, Dan, Joseph, Benjamin, Naphtali, Gad, and Asher. The sons of Judah with Tamar his daughter-in-law baring him Perez and Zerah. King David's lineage as follows:

Sons of Perez: Hezron, Hamul. The sons of Zerah: Zimri, Ethan, Heman, Calcol, Dara. The son of Ethan: Azariah. The sons of Hezron: Jerahmeel, Ram, Chelubai. Ram father of Amminadab, son is Nahshon, his son Salma became father of Boaz, his son Obed, and Obed father of Jesse. Jesse father of Eliab, Abinadab, Shimea, Nethanel, Raddai, Ozem, David, sisters are Zeruiah and Abigail. Zeruiah sons are Abishai, Joab, Asahel. Abigail bore Amasa who was the father of Jether. (1ˢᵗ Chrn. 2:5-17)

Sons of Ezrah: Jether, Mered, Epher and Jalon: She bore Miriam, Shammai and Ishbah father of Eshtemoa. His wife a Jewess bore Jered father of Gedor, Heber father of Soco, and Jekuthiel father of Zanoah. (1ˢᵗ Chrn. 4:17) Samson was of Eshtemoa.

"These are the heads of their fathers' houses. The sons of Reuben the firstborn of Israel: Hanoch, Pallu, Hezron, and Carmi; these are the families of Reuben.

The sons of Simeon: Jemuel, and Jamin, and Obad, and Jachin, and Zohar, and Shaul the sons of a Canaanite woman; these are the families of Simeon.

These are the names of the sons of Levi according to their generations: Gershom, Kohath and Merari; and the years of the life of Levi were on hundred thirty-seven years.

The sons of Gershom: Libni and Shimei, according to their families.

The sons of Kohath: Amram, and Izhar, and Hebron, and Uzziel; and the years of the life of Kohath were on hundred thirty-three years.

The sons of Merari: Mahli and Mushi." (Ex. 6:14-19)

"Amram took Jochebed the father's sister to himself as wife; and she bore him Aaron and Moses. The years of the life of Amram were one hundred thirty-seven years.

The sons of Izhar: Korah, and Nepheg, and Zichri. The sons of Uzziel, Mishael, and Elzaphan, and Sithri.

Aaron took Elisheba, the daughter of Amminadab, the sister of Nahshon, as his wife, and she bore him Nadab and Abihu, Eleazar, and Abiasaph; these are the families of the Korahites. Elisheba is Hebrew for Elizabeth. Sons of Korah: Assir, Elkanah, Abiasaph. Eleazar Aaron's son took one of the daughter of Putiel as his wife, and she bore him Phinehas." (Ex. 6:20-25)

Miriam the prophetess, the sister of Aaron, took a tambourine in her hand; and all the women went out after her with tambourines and with dances. Miriam answered them, "Sing to Yahweh, for he has triumphed gloriously." (Ex. 15:20-21)

"Then **Moses, Aaron, Nadab, Abihu, and seventy of the elders of Israel went up. They saw the God of Israel**. Under his feet was like a **paved work of sapphire stone**, like the skies for clearness." (Ex. 24:9) They made **the Ark of acacia wood and a veil of blue, and purple, and scarlet**, and fine twined linen, with cherubim. (Ex. 25:10, 26:31) "You shall make a **plate of pure gold, and engrave on it**, like the **engravings of a signet, 'Holy to Yahweh.'** (Ex. 28:36)

CHAPTER FOUR

BIBLICAL TIMELINE

The next several pages I took from my previous **copyrighted book,** **"I AM Amen Yahweh Yashar'El Your Savior, Your King,"** to let you understand the truth, and the significance of history.

Even though the Book of Daniel was written between 167-164 BCE does not mean that Daniel lived during that time period. The fact is that Daniel is the second son of King David. (1st Chrn. 3:2, Ezra 8:1-3). **Daniel is also known as Chileab, and is second son of David by Abigail** former wife of Nabal. (1st Sam. 3:2-5) In Old Testament there are unique names mentioned that can only relate to the dates and times those individual people lived: Samuel, David, Daniel, Absalom, and Solomon.

Daniel, the son of David was taken to Babylon, and was renamed to be Belteshazzar in the time of Nebuchadnezzar, in the reign of Jehoiakim King of Judah.

Daniel was actually deported earlier with invasion of the Assyrians and King Pul of Assyria. (1st Chrn. 5:26) He remained in Babylon until the return of the exiles. See my timeline of events in my previous book, "I Am Amen Yahweh Yashar'El Your Savior, Your King", to establish the years the exiles returned. There is a reference to, not only, Daniel being son of David, but when he came out of Babylon with heads of families. (Ezra. 8:1-3) Pay attention to the people in the timeline of history.

"These with their genealogies are the heads of families who set out from Babylon with me in the reign of King Artaxerxes: of the sons of **Phinehas: Gershom**; of the sons of Ithamar: **Daniel; of the sons of David:** Hattush son of Shecaniah of the sons of Parosh: **Zechariah..**" (Ezra 8:1-3) "Daniel remained there until the first year of King Cyrus." (Dan. 1:21)

Just in the reference to the genealogies is mentioned **Phinehas who is the son of Eleazar and grandson of Aaron and Gershom who is the son of Levi, and Daniel the son of King David**. (Num. 3:17) "And this is the sign to you, that which will befall your two sons, Hophni and Phinehas;...(1ˢᵗ Samuel 4:11) The Levites – Levi's sons: Gershom Kohath, and Merari. Kohath's....his son Phinehas, his son Abishua.." (1ˢᵗ Chrn. 6:50)

In order to understand the difference in years of the events, and people is due to the different calendars being used, and the calculations for timeline of events. There was Hebrew Anno Mundi (A.M.) which is year of Creation, the Hebrew Lunar Calendar or called Jewish Calendar, and Egyptian, Greek, and Babylonian Calendars to Gregorian. For instance according to Hebrew Calendar the year world created was 5776 A.M. Kingdom of Greeks 1000BCE.

To further clarify the actual timeline, the Book of Daniel was written between 167-164BCE, or time period of 850 BCE. That date perimeter of 167 BCE does not mean that this is when Daniel lived, or when events occurred for it **references the kingdom of the Greeks which started in 1000BCE. So if you take the date of 167 and subtract it from 1000=833 BCE.**

For instance Daniel was placed in the lions pit, and God told Habbakuk to take the stew he made and give it to Daniel. "Take the meal you are carrying to Babylon and give it to Daniel in Lions pit." (Dan. 14:34) The **prophet Habakkuk was son of Shioua Lovit,** and his **mother is Lesho Namit the Shunammite woman in time of Elisha.**-(2ⁿᵈ Kgs. 4:12-17)

Elisha was with Elijah the Tishbite and Obadiah in the time of Ahab King of Israel. (1ˢᵗ Kgs. 17:1) Elisha son of Shaphat.(2ⁿᵈ Kgs. 3:11)

In the Book of Daniel it states: "It was the first year of Darius son of Ahasuerus, who was of Median stock and ruled the kingdom of Chaldea. In the first year of his reign, I, Daniel, was pursuing the Scriptures, counting over the number of years – as revealed by Yahweh **to the prophet Jeremiah – that were to pass before the successive devastation of Jerusalem would come to a end,** namely **seventy years.**" (Dan. 9:1-3)

The first deportation from Jerusalem occurred during the time of Nebuchadnezzar king of Babylon during reign of Jehoiakim. However, there were previous deportations to Babylon other then the time of Pul of Assyria in 799 BCE. The time frame of events with people involved becomes a definite correlation to time of which Daniel, the son of David lived 879.

Elijah was proclaiming to make the paths straight for the upright one which is Yashar'El as contained in the Book of the Just which was referenced in the Books of Joshua and Samuel. "In the fifteenth year of Amaziah son of Joash, King of Judah, Jeroboam son of Joash became King of Israel in Samaria..." (2 Kgs. 14:1, 23)

Most people didn't realize that Daniel from the Book of Daniel, was actually King David's son, and that there have been many invasions during the course of history.

Within this chapter please note that the prophet's mentioned were **Habbakkuk, Jeremiah, Zechariah, Elijah, as well as, Jehoiakim or spelled Joiakim.** This is very important for that puts these people in the years of 879 BCE to at least to 799BCE. **Isaiah started prophesying around 849 BCE.**

I know it seems tedious to read excerpts of names contained in Old Testament, but that is the only way to show the lineage, and answer the question -which Zechariah was it?

Adaiah son of Jeroham, son of Pelaliah son of Amzi, son of **Zechariah**, son of Pashur, son of Malchijah." (Neh. 11:12) **Elijah was a brother of Zechariah,** and Adaiah of the **sons of Jeroham.**

Asaph brother of Heman, and Zechariah. (1st Chrn. 6:39, 16:5) **Asaph son of Berechiah, son of Shimea,** son of **Michael,** son of Baaseiah, son of **Malchijah,** son of Ethni, son of Zerah, son of Adaiah, son **of Ethan,** of Zimmah, son of **Shimei,** of Jahath, of Gershom, **of Levi.** (1st Chrn. 6:39-43) **Of Gershom-Libni,** Johath, Zimnah, **Joah, Iddo,** Zerah, **Amminadab son Korah, son is Assir, Elkanah.** (1st Chrn. 6:20-21) His son Ebiasaph, son **Assir,** Tanath, Uriel, his son **Uzziah, his son Shaul.** (1st Chrn. 6:22-24)

Sometimes to see the actual dates of events, and what occurred with the people involved, helps to clarify the timeline of history. This chart is similar to the chart from my copyrighted work contained in my other book, "I Am Amen Yahweh Yashar'El, Your Savior, Your King." So I listed part of the dates of history from my other book as follows:

870	**David anointed King of Israel by Samuel which united Israel** "In those days the House of **Judah will unite with the House of Israel.**" (Jer. 3:18) The rebellion ends around 843.3-6.3=837
	David reigned for 33 years. Solomon born in Jerusalem
	David nominated the Cantor. Sons of Kohath: Heman son of Joel, son of Samuel of Elkanah, of Azariah, of Zephaniah. His brother Asaph son of Berechiah... sons of Merari: Ethan- sons of Amaziah, son of Hilkiah of Mushi of Merari of Levi. (1st Chrn. 6:16-31)
	Junior cantors to kinsmen: sons of Asaph, Joseph...For Heman: Bukkiah, Mattaniah, Uzziel..(1st Chrn. 25:4) **Elijah son of Jeroham** (1st Chrn. 8:26-27) Isaiah son of Amoz- (Is. 1:1, 2nd Chrn. 26:22)
	King David's military and civil commissioners assigned to: Banaiah champion of the 30; Elihu one of David's brothers, son of Obadiah Ishmaiah, Hoshea son of Amaziah, Joel son of Pedaiah, Iddo son of Zechariah...Jonathan David's uncle. (1st Chrn. 27:5, 18, 19-21, 32) Victory over Jebusites capture of Jerusalem & Philistines (2nd Sam. 5:6, 17)
867	**Elkanah was killed** (2nd Chrn. 28:7-8) during Aramaean war.
	Time of **Ahaziah of Attaiah, son of Uzziah son of Zechariah** (Neh. 11:4-9) time of Jehoram, son of Jehoshaphat (2nd Chen. 21:2) son of Ahaziah son of Jehoram (2nd Chrn. 22:1) Jehoshaphat son of Ahilud (2nd Sam. 20:24)

836	census **Mary and Joseph**
837 Tishri	**The Keystone laid by King David YHWH Star of David**
Sept. 25th	**Tishri=Month of Creation and Feast of Tabernacles**
837-797	at age 12 Solomon becomes King reigns 40 years
833	The Temple building started in 4th year reign of Solomon
826	**Temple Completed took seven years to complete "Yet will God really live with men on earth?"** (2nd Chrn. 6:18)
797/798	Solomon dies at age 52 **Haggai son of Shealtiel son of Solomon** "..and my **spirit remains among you.**" (Haggai 1:15, 2:4-5) "..from the **twenty-fourth day of ninth month, from the day the foundations of the sanctuary of Yahweh was laid..**" (Haggai 2:18-19) Hezekiah
849-837 ****	**Song of Immanuel Isaiah, Zechariah, Micah, Amos Isaiah** son of Amoz- (Is.1:1, 2nd Chrn 26:22) **837+12=849 and 849-12=837**
****	**Hosea/Osee son of Beeri in days of Uzziah, Jotham, Ahaz and Hezekiah kings of Judah in the days of Jeroboam son of Joash king of Israel-**(2nd Kgs 14:23, Hosea 1:1) **Elijah** and **Elisha**-(2nd Kgs. 2:12) **Hebrew Book of Osee "your mother the synagogue"**2:2 (Book of Tobit 1:1-9, 5:14-19) Tobit proclaimed "..**the name of Her who is Elect shall endure through the generations to come.**" (Tobit 13:11-14) "..**gates of Jerusalem shall be built of Sapphire...**" (Tobit 13:20-23) Tobit died 112 yrs. old and a **census was taken of Jews living in Israel for they will be exiled** to different territories, and territory of Israel and **Jerusalem will be a desert.** Then God will take pity on them and bring them back to land of Israel. (Tobit 14:5-6)

| 867-799 | Absalom given name of Pillar of Absalom when seven of them perished together, they were put to death in the days of the barley harvest. (2nd Sam.18:18, 21:9) Manasseh died in the barley harvest. Mattathias is the son of Absalom-(1st Macc.11:70 webc, 2nd Samuel) |
| **** | |

Jonathan son of Absalom (1st Macc. 13:9-11 webc)
Simon his brother (1st Macc 13:25-30webc)
Habakkuk son of Joshua carried meal to Daniel in Babylon while in the lions den in Babylon. Daniel was 80 years old at time.
***879-80=799 80 years old Daniel**
Martyrdom of seven brothers (Jer. 15:9, 2nd Macc. 7:1-42 webc)
Antiochus eve of Mordecai and Jeremiah (2nd Macc. 15:15, 36webc)
Rebellion Ends 843 (2nd Sam. 20:14-26)**The mother of seven sons Jeremiah's referenced as his mother.** (Jer. 15:9-10)

796-780	Rehoboam son of Solomon King in Judah
	Asa King Judah Elijah and Elisha and Obadiah, Ahab
	Maacah mother of Asa she is daughter of Absalom-(2nd Chrn. 11:20, 15:16)

| 782 | Jehoshaphat son of Asa (2nd Chrn. 17:1) spread true religion (2nd Chr. 18:10 |

| 797/798 | Jeroboam was King in Israel son is **Zechariah time of Hezekiah** 798 |

| 797 | Joash of King of Israel (2nd Kgs 12:20-21) same time Amaziah King Judah |
| | Amaziah father of Uzziah |

849-782	**Uzziah also called Azariah/Azarias-Tobit son of Ananiel who's mother was Deborah as well as kinsmen to Azarias.**
	Hilkiah son is Azariah- (1st Chrn. 9:11) priest Solomon's Temple (1st Chrn. 5:40)
	Judith time of Uzziah chief, and **Joakim** high priest. (Judith 4:6, 11 7:23, 8:9) and Hezekiah, Isaiah
	Elijah is listed as son of Jeroham -(1st Chrn. 8:26-27)

794/792****	time of Jeroboam II is **Jonah** (2nd Kgs 14:25) and Amos. Jonah's father is Amittai -(2nd Kgs. 14:25) **792+45=837**
783	Joash of Judah reign begins at 7 years of age (2nd Kgs. 11:21)
779	Abijah
766	Ahaz King Judah and Ahab King Israel before Elijah ascended Aramaens invaded during reign of Ahaz .King Pul Tiglath-Pilser Assyria
750-721	**Hezekiah son of Ahaz of Judah/Manasseh his son co-regent. Hosea, and Nahum the prophets. Nathan son of Nahum of David** (2nd Kgs 19:35) **Sennacherib invasion** (2nd Chrn. 32:1-8) **Nicanor was with Sennacherib** (2nd Macc. 15:23-25) **Hezekiah builds walls** that were broken
721 ***	**Manasseh** reign 719/721 Merodoch Baladon (Is. 39:1) **Judith wife of Manasseh with Joakim high priest and Ezekial Holofernes of Assyria**
746	Ezekial marked cross on foreheads in Jerusalem all who deployed evil. (Ezk. 9:4-5) "I mean to reduce the country to a desert.." (Ezk. 15:1-8)
747-722/723	**Hoshea last king of Israel son of Elah of Beeri he is listed with Judith**
721/722**	**Jehozadak son of Azariah, of Hilkiah who was carried off by Nebuchadnezzer-1st Chrn. 5:39-40**
722-729**	**Israel exiled to Assyria by Shalmaneser V time of Hoshea**

729/542***	**return of exiles after 70 years** Zech. 1:13
	the Jews working to restore walls, the foundations already laid. Ez. 4:12
	***799-729=70 years Tobit said** exiled to different territories before bringing them home to Jerusalem. Time Pul exiled them to Assyria 799 Prophets Haggai, Zechariah son of Iddo
	Zerrubable son of Shealtiel and Jeshua, son of Jozadak started to build Temple in Jerusalem Ez. 5:1-2
665-634	**Josiah King Judah son of Amon of Manasseh 1ˢᵗ Chrn. 3:13-14**
	2ⁿᵈ Chrn 34 was 8 years old and reigned 31 years in Jerusalem and **placed Ark 22 years before Destruction of Temple** worked on repairing the Temple and **Hilkiah found book of law.**
	2ⁿᵈ Chrn. 34:1, 34:9-10, 34:14-15, 35:3
	Josiah's sons: Johanan, Jehoiakim, Zedekiah, Shallum. 1ˢᵗ Chrn. 3:14-16
647	**The Passover was celebrated in 18ᵗʰ year of his reign**, and then latter killed by Neco king of Egypt at Megiddo. 2ⁿᵈ Chr. 35:19-23 Jer. 46:2-3
634	Jehoiakim son of Jeshua reigned. 11 year son is Jehoiachin/Jeconiah
623	Jeconiah King of Juda son of Jehoiakim reigned 3 months 10 days
	time of Esther and Mordecai – the day of Adar and Nicanor 2ⁿᵈ Macc 15:35-36 Ahasuerus. Cambyses=Xerxes husband of Esther 626 beginning of reign of **Xerxes also known as Ahasuerus** Jewish History from Greek texts Xerexs 626. see Bk Esther **Cyrus** 600 BCE
623 ***	Jeremiah of Libnah was son of Hilkiah. 2 Kngs. 23:31, 24:18
	Habakkuk in Jerusalem **11 years before the** destruction of Temple.

CHAPTER FIVE

HISTORY OF MACCABEES

In order to understand the timeline of different books was to place the people involved within those events. For instance in the Book of Maccabees the years were listed, however, within the first book (1st Macc. 1:10-12 webc) stated one hundred and thirty-seventh year of the kingdom of the Greeks.

To state kingdom of Greeks was very important for the **Kingdom of Greeks started around 1000 BCE-336 BCE. So the date of 137 is subtracted from 1000=863 BCE.**

Absalom was the son of King David and the wars and rebellion were contained within that time frame 867-837 BCE, in the time of Maccabees.

Alexander the first from Hellene Greece began the Hellenistic era 1000-336 BCE. It was after his death that the empire was divided into three parts of city states:

Antigonid which covered Greece, Macedonia, Sparta, Seleucid which covered Mesopotamia, Anatolia, Syria, Levant, Persia to Indian territory, Ptolemaic which is Egypt. Ptolemy Soter was general in Alexander's army, and took over Egypt after his death. **Antiochus is the son of Soter.** (Dan. 11:8, 42)

Homer of Greece wrote the Iliad 800 BCE with the Trojan war with Hector and Paris of Troy fighting Menelaus of Sparta. The war was started when Paris took Menelaus wife Helen to Troy. **Menelaus was listed in the Book of Maccabees as well as Jonathan sending a letter to Menelaus of Sparta.** (2nd Macc. Chapter 4, 13:3 webc)

Hector and Paris are the sons of King Priam and Queen Hecuba of Troy. **Paris because of his intelligence earned the surname of Alexander.**

Jason is the son of Simon the brother of Onias which Menelaus supplanted.

Lysimachus was the brother of Menelaus. (2nd Macc. 4:27-49 webc)

Cleopatra of Macedonia is the sister of Alexander the Great. **King Phillip appointed Alexander the brother of Olympias as King of Molossis.** Cleopatra is also the daughter of King Philip of Macedonia and Queen Olympias. Philip married a woman named Cleopatra the daughter of Attalus from Macedonia. Olympias went into exile when Philip married Cleopatra to Alexander of Molossis the brother of Olympias. Cleopatra the daughter of Ptolemy left Egypt to marry Alexander. (1st Macc. 10:51-60 webc)

Judas son of Chalphi the general of the army. (1st Macc. 11:70 webc)

Aristobolus is the grandson of Maccabeus, and Absalom is both uncle and father-in-law to Aristobolus. Aristobolus in Hebrew means Jonathan. Alexander's eldest son is Aristobolus II, and son-in-law of Hycranus. **John Hycranus is the son of Tobias the son of Tobit of Simeon.** (2nd Macc. 3:11 webc, also see Book of Tobit)

Alexander's trusted officer was Antipater. When **Antipater died, the general Antigonus Monphthalmus** ordered the murder of Cleopatra. **Antigonus II in Hebrew is Mattathias.**

Mattithias Maccabeus. (2nd Macc. 6:18, 7:1-42 webc, Jer. 15:5)

Judas also called Maccabeus (1st Macc. 3:1 webc) Mattathias is the father of the Maccabees. In New Testament they refer to **Cleopas as the husband of Martha**, but in other referenced sources he is the brother of **Mattathias. In Jewish history Simeon surname is Cleopas. Mattithias was father of Maccabees, and is the son of Absalom.** (1st Macc. 11:70 webc)

*****So Mariah, the sister of Mary, was married to either Shimeon one of the sons of Harim,** (Ez. 10:31) Or the wife of Simon the son of Mattithias of Absalom the grandson of Simeon.

Absalom was Ambassador to Lysias. (2nd Macc. 11:17 webc) **Claudius Lysias was the governor of Syria. Simon was the son of Mattathias the son of Absalom.** (1st Macc 11:70 webc)

******Jonathan is son of Absalom.** (1st Macc. 13:9-11 webc)

Judas was the brother to Simon and Jonathan. (1st Macc. 5:17-18 webc) **Joseph was the son of Zechariah of Azariah.** (1st Macc. 5:17-18 webc) and **Azariah was with Daniel, son of David in Babylon.** (Dan. 1:8) Eleazar is called Avaran (1st Macc. 6:43-44 webc) and **Jason is the son of Eleazar.** (1st Macc. 8:17-18webc) **Eleazar son of Phinehas.** (1st Chrn. 9:20 2nd Sam. 18:17, 9:10) son of **Dodo** (2nd Sam. 23:9) **son of Joash** who was **commissioner** for cattle by King David. (1st Chrn. 27:29)

******Eleazar at age 90 was martyred along with seven brothers.**

"The country was at peace throughout days of Simon." (1st Macc. 14:1-4 webc)

"Each man sat under his own vine and his own fig tree." (1st Macc. 14:12 webc, Jer. 24 chapter Micah 4:4) **Micah is the son of Joel** (1st Chrn. 5:4-7)

Abubus is the son-in-law of Simon Maccabeus and father of Ptolemeus. (1st Macc. 16:11, 26:11 webc)

Dositheus was captain of Judas Maccabeus and then **Dositheus and Sosipater generals** (2nd Macc. 12: 19-20 webc) Dositheus one of the Tubians who grasped Gorgias cloak. (2nd Macc. 12:35-46 webc, Book of Esther 10:13-14)

Seleucus is Philopater King of Asia and son of Antiochus great. (2nd Macc. 4:7-8, 18-13 webc)

Sennecherib and Nicanor time of Simon, Joseph, Jonathan who were ready to die for the laws and their country. (2nd Macc. 8:8-24 webc)

"This day of the purification of the Temple fell on the very day on which the Temple had been profaned by the foreigners, the twenty-fifth of the same month, Chislev. They kept eight festal days with rejoicing, in the manner of the Feast of Tabernacles."

(2nd Macc. 10:5-6 webc) So the Kingdom of Greeks the **163 year of Greek is 837 BCE. Jeremiah conceals the tabernacle, ark and altar.** (2nd Macc. 2:1-12webc, Book of Jeremiah) Simon and his sons Mattathias and Judas were murdered by Ptolemy military commissioner **plane of Jericho** Greek year 177, or year 823, and then went to find John to inform him that his father and brothers were murdered. **Recorded in Acts of John.** (1st Macc. 16:23 webc)

Mattathias son of John, son of **Simeon priest of sons of Joarib.** (1st Macc. 2:1) and son of Absalom (1st Macc. 11:70 webc, 2nd Sam.) Had five sons John, Simon, Judas and Eleazar, Jonathan. (1st Macc. 2:3-6 webc)

Joarib or spelled Jehoiarib (1st Chrn. 24:7) Of the **priests in Jerusalem: Jedaiah, Jehoiarib,** Jachin, Azariah son of Hilkiah, son of Meshullam, son of Zadok, son of Meraioth, son of Ahitub, ruler of the House of God." (1st Chrn. 9:10-12) **Phinehas son of Eleazar, Zechariah time of David before he became King.** (1st Chrn. 9:20-21) Mattathias son of John of Joiada (Neh. 12:11)

Razis elder of Jerusalem denounced by Nicanor and he was known as father of the Jews cause of his kindness. (2nd Macc. 14:37-46 webc)

Campaign of **Lysias** "Sent a good Angel to save Israel. Maccabaeus himself was the first to take up his weapons... They were still near Jerusalem when a rider attired in white appeared at their head brandishing golden accouterments..... They advanced in battle order with the aid of their celestial ally, the Lord having had mercy on them."

(2nd Macc. 11:7-11webc, also see Isaiah chapter 63) Lysias wrote to Jews saying "John and Absalom, your envoys.."(2nd Macc. 11:17 webc) see also Book of Samuel **year of Greek 148 or 852 BCE.**

Ptolemy Soter 1st was general in Alexander's army. After the death of Alexander Ptolemy Soter began the Ptolemaic kingdom. Ptolemy was originally from Macedon and he declared himself pharaoh of Egypt. All the male descendants took the name Ptolemy, and the women took the names of Cleopatra.. Ptolemy 1st along with the Seleucus the rulers of Babylonia joined forces to defeat **Demetrius**, the **son of Antigonus.**

Antigonus in Hebrew is Mattathias. (John 1:12, and Book of Maccabees)

Ptolemy Philadelphus, son of Ptolemy 1st shared rule with his father. He defeated the Kush to gain their territory. (Reference Gen. 10:6 and 1st Chrn. 1:8) **Kush or spelled Cush are the Cushites/Kushites.** (Book of Daniel 11:44)

His first wife was Arsinoe, or called Cleopatra, was the daughter of Lysimachus. (Book of Esther 11:1) **Herodotus calls himself Apries, but Greek spelling is Herodes, and Jeremiah refers to him as Hophra.** (Jer. 44:30) **Was in the time of Alexander.**

843 Rebellion (2nd Sam. 20:14-26) Even in the Book of Daniel references time lines. The reference to two thousand three hundred evenings and mornings, or **2,300 equates to 6.31 years. So the Maccabean revolt lasted 6.30 years which occurred around 843.31-837=6.31, 843.31-6.31= 837 BCE**

The coming Branch....each other sit under own fig tree...house of Josiah son of Zephaniah who has arrived from Babylon....make a crown and set it on the head of Joshua son of Jehozadak...man named Branch will rebuild the sanctuary of Yahweh. (Zech. 3:10, 6:10-12, dedication 1ˢᵗ Macc. 4:55-58 webc)

"Your fortresses are all fig trees laden with early-ripening figs..." (Nah. 3:12)

Our Lady of Mercy Blessed Mother Mary
October 8, 2006   by: Karen Sobek

CHAPTER SIX

SONG OF SONGS

Many people always classified the Books of the Prophets as Major and Minor. I consider all of them as major for their great love of God Almighty Yahweh. These books refer to the greatest event in history, and how God Yahweh came to earth himself to be our Immanuel, our Yashar'El, Our Savior.

In Song of Songs, or called the Song of Solomon, is not just the words of love, but what the words were conveying about people and timeline of events in Jerusalem. Just in the very opening segment references Kedar's tents. (Song 1:5)

This reference has different meaning. First it is to a person called Kedar who was Abraham's grandson and second son of Ishmael, and second it refers to the residue of the number of archers which were the children of Kedar. (Gen. 25:13, Is. 21:17) And third to the tents of Issachar. (Det. 33:18) Fourth would be to the Tent, and Tent Peg Of God.

These people grazed among the shepherds tents of Solomon.

"My beloved is to me a sachet of myrrh that lies between my breasts. My beloved is to me a cluster of henna blossoms from the vineyards of En Gedi." (Song 1:13-14)

This geographical reference to En Gedi is also known as a oasis on western shore of the Dead Sea, a spring, but it is also where David fled to from Saul. (Ez. 23:29. 24:2, 47:10)

Solomon used cedars from Lebanon to build the Temple in Jerusalem, and it was his father King David who selected the cornerstone and inscribed it.

"I am a rose of Sharon, a lily of the valleys. As a lily among thorns, so is my love among the daughters." (Song 2:1-2) This starts to reference the lineage of Mary for Hannah her mother is known as the Lily of the Valley. Sharon is a Mediterranean coastal region around Mount Carmel. This is a fertile plain area where they use to pasture flocks. The word thorn, is also thistle which is referred to a location called Lebanon. Hannah in Hebrew is also spelled as Channah, which means Grace, and also means Royal Lily. (Hos. 14:5)

(1st Chrn. 5:16, 27:29, Is. 33:9, 65:10) Hannah was from this area of the tribe of Asher. Lily is also used as a wedding song by the sons of Korah in Psalm 45.

The pluralism of the word "daughters" leads me to conclude that Hannah had twin daughters, Mary and Mariah, and that Mary was the chosen one to become the mother of our Savior. Hannah and Elkanah had three sons and two daughters: Samuel, Abijah, Eliezar, Mary and Mariah.

As an Apple tree is sweet to taste it also used in context to Eve, a garden, and to the Apple of my eye, a location called Jerusalem. Meaning that whoever would touch, or come against God's Holy place, would suffer the consequences of that action. (Zech. 2:8)

The **apple** trees blossom and bear fruit in **September same month of our Savior's birth.** "He surrounded him. He cared for him. He kept him as the apple of his eye." (Det. 12:10)

The Temple of Yahweh was built and surrounded by a wall and lattices were on the window openings where they looked through waiting on the chariot to come. (Judges 5:28, 1st Kg. 6:4) The Chariot of God (Ps. 68:17 and Ez. 1:4-28)

The **fig tree ripens** during the months of July-November, and are good figs. (Is. 28:4, Jer. 24:2, 3, Hos. 9:10) With the **main crop** being in **August and September**. (1st Samuel 25:18)

The deer on the mountains of Bether from (Song 2:17) is also mentioned in the Book of Joshua (Jos. 15:59) This is a geographical location not far from Jerusalem. (Jer. 34:18-19) From the flock which came from the washing, and everyone has twins is reference to twins of Jacob and Esau, but also to the twin brothers called Perez and Zerah. Gen. 38:29-3) Perez is the lineage of Hannah of Asher, and I believe gave birth to twin daughters, Mary and Mariah. The scarlet thread or the lineage in which they came from is also referenced to Perez and Zerah for the midwife put a scarlet thread on the first baby's hand. So the thread is from Perez to Asher which is lineage of Hannah, who's husband is Elkanah, the parents of Mariah and Mary to Our Savior, Our Immanuel. Also the priests linen cloth would be sewn with gold, blue, purple and scarlet thread. (Ex. 28:5) The thread of High Priests in the lineage.

The Temples are like pomegranate which is a fruit that is in abundance during the autumn season. This gives another reference to time of year for the first day of Autumn which is September 25th.

In chapter four of the Song is referring to Temple Mount where the Temple is located, and the Ark is within the Holy of Holies. The Tabernacle was separated by the veil which was placed before the Holy of Holies and contains the Ark of the Covenant. (Ex. 26:31-35, Heb. 10:19-22) This veil was a partition before God through which only the High Priest could enter.

Pomegranates are used in the decoration of the pillar capitals. Pomegranate also was woven into the robe worn by the High Priests. (Ex. 28:33-34) According to Jewish tradition it also **symbolizes righteousness.**

Righteousness is also represented by the word Yashar, Yasharun, or spelled Jeshurun, meaning the upright one, or righteous one, from the Book of the Just.

(see Joshua and Samuel, Det. 33:26)

The tower of David is the Citadel located near the Jaffa Gate on the western side of Jerusalem facing west. There are eight gates in the city walls with four main gates being:

Jaffa Gate, Damascus Gate, **Lion's Gate and Zion Gate**. The **Golden Gate which faces east** is the **Gate which Yahweh our Savior enters.** The Zion Gate, or known as David's Gate, is located on Mount Zion. From the tower of Ramleh you can see the Plain of Sharon, which is the area from which Hannah, the Lily of the Valley lived, and is south of Lebanon.

The flock feeds among the Lilies. The Lion Gate is reference to the scepter that is of Judah. (Gen. 49:6-10) From Judah is also the choice vine of grapes. "Binding his foal to the vine; he has washed his garments in wine, his robes in the blood of the grapes. His eyes will be red with wine his teeth white with milk." (Gen. 49:11-13) The sons of Israel referenced are Judah, Asher who is Royal, and Joseph the vine. Hannah was from the tribe of Asher.

"Look from the top of Amana, from the top of Senir and Hermon, from the lions dens, from the mountains of the leopards." (Song 4:8)

Amana is a ancient name for southern Anti-Lebanon mountains. In ancient history the land of Canaan was from the Jordan River to the Mediterranean Sea, and within this land area contains Mount Hermon which is the highest mountain in Israel. (Ps. 89:13) Shenir is also spelled Mount Shenir. In this area of Lebanon was wolves, leopards and lions of the forest which could harm them. (Is. 11:6, Jer. 5:6, 13:23, Dan. 7:6, Hosea 13:7, Habakkuk 1:8)

But it also pertains to the sons of Israel. Zebulon dwells by the sea, and Benjamin a wolf. (Gen. 49:13, 27)

"...a fountain of gardens, a well of living waters." (Song 4:15) This references that God once had a Garden in Eden, a vineyard in Baal Hamon as in Jerusalem. (Gen. 2:8, Song 8:11)

God Yahweh is the living water of life, and that a fountain shall flow out of Yahweh's house. (Joel 3:18)

In the line, "His cheeks are like a bed of spices with towers of perfumes. His lips are like lilies, dropping liquid myrrh. His hands are like rings of gold set with beryl. His body is like ivory work overlaid with sapphires. His legs are like pillars of marble set on sockets of fine gold." (Song 5:13-15) Is a description of the Ark of the Covenant. It is also pointing to the genealogy of Hannah and Mary with reference to lilies. The perfumes and spices were used in the Temple as incense, and Sapphire is also relating to the month of September.

"Then **Moses, Aaron, Nadab, Abihu, and seventy of the elders of Israel went up. They saw the God of Israel.** Under his feet was like a **paved work of sapphire stone**, like the skies for clearness." (Ex. 24:9) They made **the Ark of acacia wood and a veil of blue, and purple, and scarlet**, and fine twined linen, with cherubim. (Ex. 25:10, 26:31) "You shall make a **plate of pure gold, and engrave on it**, like the **engravings of a signet, 'Holy to Yahweh.'** (Ex. 28:36) The **tetragammaton of Yahweh is YHWH.**

In Chapter Six Tirzah is Hebrew word meaning "my delight" and refers to the daughters of Zelophehad. It is also a city which Joshua conquered. (Jos. 12:24) Zelophehad is the mother of five daughters: Mahlah, Noa, Hoglah, Milcah and Tirzah. (Num. 27:1-2)

"Along the side of Gilead". (Song 6:5)

These daughters were of the son of Hepher, of Gilead, son of Machir, the son of Manasseh. "They stood before Moses, before Eleazar the priest.." (Num. 27:1-2)

The name Shulammite means Peaceable Perfect in Hebrew, and that Shulammite, as at the dance of Mahanaim. In Hebrew Mahanaim means she danced between two camps.

The pools of Heshbon was a fishing area with a stream underneath. In the books of Numbers, Deuteronomy it was the capital of Amorites. The Israelites won the war with the Amorites in the time of the Exodus with Moses. (Num. 21:25, Jos. 3:10, 17, Det. 2:24, 29:7)

This city Heshbon is located due East of Jerusalem, and it was where the Israelites entered the Promised Land. This geographical location was assigned to the Tribe of Gad.

"Under the apple tree I aroused you, there your mother conceived you, there she was in labor and bore you. Set me as a seal on your heart, as a seal on your arm; for love is strong as death.....Many waters can't quench love, neither can floods drown it. If a man would give all the wealth of his house for love." (Song 8:5-7)

Jerusalem is built with a wall around it, and with turrets, ramparts, and towers.

"Solomon had a vineyard at Baal Hamon" (Song 8:11) "You who dwell in the gardens, with friends in attendance, let me hear your voice." (Song 8:13) "From the remotest earth we **hear songs, "Honor to the upright one**." (Is. 24:14-16) Upright one is Yashar 'El.

CHAPTER SEVEN

ISAIAH

In the Book of Isaiah contains very important information to the events in history. Isaiah actually started his prophesying around 849 BCE. It was Isaiah who wrote the announcement of the coming of the Messiah, as contained in the Song of Immanuel. Elijah was prophesying even before Isaiah to make a straight highway across the desert for the upright one. The very reference to "upright one" is referring to the Book of the Just, Yashar. Isaiah was the son of Amoz. Amoz's brother was Amaziah brother of Azariah who latter became King. So Isaiah was the nephew of Azariah. And Zechariah's son was Uzziah. (Gen. 38:26-30)

Most people think only in terms of Kings, or Queens, instead of looking at the people, and who they are in certain period of time. For instance, in the opening lines of the Book of Isaiah it states that he is the son of Amoz, and in Jerusalem in days of Uzziah, Jotham, Ahaz, and Hezekiah. Amoz was the brother of Amaziah, of Hilkiah, who was the son of Shallum of Zadok. This Uzziah, referred by others as Azariah was of great age, was a leper was in the time perimeter of 782 BCE. However before Uzziah became King he was in the time of King David which puts him, as well as Elijah, Zechariah, Azariah, Hilkiah, Uzziah, Heman, Joiarib, Amaziah, and others during the time period beginning around 869 BCE.

(1st Chrn. 6:16-31, 8:26-27, 25:2-22, 27:5, 18,19-21, 32, 2nd Chrn.26:23)

This Uzziah's father was Amaziah, and he was the son of Joash, which is one of the sons of Becher of Benjamin. (1st Chrn. 7:6-8) Also Uzziah was the son of Zechariah, son of Jeroham, and also known as Azariah.

What further illustrates that these people were in Jerusalem at time of King David at least 100 years earlier in time is that Gideon is also the son of Joash. David was born 907/908 BCE. (Judges 6:11, 30, 8:32, 1st Samuel 12:11, Isaiah 9:4; 10:26) Gideon lived around 1000 BCE. However, **Uzziah was also the son of Zechariah**, the son of Amariah, son of Shephatiah, son of Mahalalel of the children of Perez. (Gen. 38:26-30) Uzziah was the son of Uriel of Tanath, and to others sons of to Assir of Korah. (1st Chr. 6:22-25) Joash was commissioner for cattle in time of King David. (1st Chrn. 27:28-29, Neh. 11:4)

Jotham son of Uzziah (Azariah) mother's name was Jerusha daughter of Zadok. (2nd Kgs. 15:32-33) Hilkiah's father Shallum was son of Zadok. (1st Chrn. 6:12-13) Hezekiah son of Ahaz and his mother's name is Abi daughter of Zechariah. (2nd Kgs. 18:1-2 2nd Chrn. 29:1)

Zadok son of Ahitub. (1st Chrn. 6:8, 2nd Samuel 8:17) Zadok father of Shallum son of Hilkiah. (2nd Chr. 6:12-13) Eliakim is son of Hilkiah. (2nd Kgs. 18:18)

Joah is the son of Asaph the recorder in David's administration. (2nd Kgs. 18:37)

Isaiah is son of Amoz of Amaziah and Hezekiah is the of son of Ahaz. (2nd Kgs. 18:1 19:2, (1st Chrn. 4:35)

Of Jeroham his sons: Elijah, Asaph, Zichri, Adaiah, Elkanah, Zechariah, Heman. Hannah the mother of Mary, and Mariah were relatives to Zechariah. (1st Chrn. 7:30-31, 8:27, 9:10-16)

Hannah wife of Elkanah, daughter of Penuel, son of Sheshak of Beriah, and his daughter Sheerah (Sarah) of Asher. (1st Chr. 7:30-38, 8:25, 4:4, Num. 26:46, 1st Chrn. 7:24)

I took these biblical references to make you understand the timeline of history, but also the background of Isaiah's life. These people actually lived in the time of King David, and his son Solomon. Which puts these people in the right year, and at the right time for the greatest event in history, the birth of Our Immanuel, Our Savior.

"....in the days of Uzziah King of Judah. Yahweh your God will come...." (Zech. 14:5) "And Yahweh will be king of the whole world. When that day comes, Yahweh will be unique and his name unique." (Zech. 14:9-10) Even though it was written "Uzziah King For there is a deviation of 10 to 100 years in history. So if Uzziah was of great age and became King, according to Assyrian records in year 782 BCE, the Hebrew timeline would be earlier putting the date between 849/791 BCE. However, there is another Uzziah son of Zechariah. King Uzziah was 16 years old when he came to the throne, so in other references him being of great age, makes it another person called Uzziah, the son of Zechariah.

Zechariah was of great age, according to New Testament, with his son being John. Zachariah is of the division of Abijah (which Abijah is the son of Samuel of Elkanah). Adaiah son of Jeroham, son of Peleliah son of Amzi, son of Zechariah, son of Pashur, son of Malchijah." (Neh. 11:12) Elijah was a brother of Zechariah, and Elkanah of the sons of Jeroham. (1st Chrn. 6:27, 39, 8:20-21, 9:12, 15:17-18, 16:5, 7:30-31, 9:10-16, 26:5, 27:2, 21-22 and 2nd Chrn. 23:1-3)

Zechariah's son Uzziah, his son is Athaiah with his son being Ahaziah. Joash is the son of Ahaziah, and Abi the daughter of Zechariah is the wife of Ahaz. (2nd Kg. 18:1-2, 15:1-2) Ahaziah the son of Jeroham. Joash is the son-in-law of Zechariah, and his daughter is Abi, which is short for Abijah.

Elijah was also in the time of King David, which establishes, not only, the mother of Mary and lineage, but to the real time frame of the birth of her son, our Immanuel, our Savior, Yashar'El, Yahweh. Elijah was one of the sons of Jeroham. (1st Chrn. 8:26-27)

In Hebrew the meaning of the **name of Elijah** has its origin in **Eliyyahu meaning "my God is Yahweh."** It was Elijah who proclaimed to make a straight highway for God. (Is. 40:3) "I am Yahweh, there is no other savior but me." (Is. 43:11)

In Hebrew the name Messiah means Holy Annointed King or Priest. Immanuel in Hebrew transliteration of the name means:

IM=I Am, Man=creation, U=Tent Peg, El=God

"I drive him like a **peg** into a firm place; he will become a throne of glory for his father's house." (Is. 23) Or in Zechariah "From him will issue **cornerstone** and **tent peg**.' (Zech. 10:4 also ref. Judges 5:26)

"Let me sing, I pray you, for my beloved, a song as to his vineyard.... My beloved hath a vineyard in a fruitful hill..." (Is. 5:1) This is referring to the Temple Mount and Solomon, which correlates to the Song of Songs.

There has been many incursions on Israel by Philistines and Assyrians, not just in the middle of the century, but during the time of David. (See Books of Samuel)

Even Tyre was left for a desert for 70 years while a remnant remained in Jerusalem. (Is. 23:15)

During this time period is when the real deportations began, and Daniel the son of David was deported. When Solomon began to reign and build the Temple, Uzziah, and Zechariah were priests and princes, with Isaiah being the nephew of Amaziah. This Zechariah was the son of Berechiah, and son of Jeroham. Uriah was priest and Jeroham's son is Zechariah. Zechariah's son Uzziah with his sons Athaiah, his son Joiarib with his son being Jedaiah of the sons of Perez. These people lived in the time of David and Solomon.

(Neh. 8:4, 11:3-7, 10-12, Is. 8:2)

At this time Isaiah relates the Song of Immanuel. "It will reach even to the neck. The stretching out of its **wings will fill the width of your land Immanuel.**" (Is. 8:8)

They were told not to be afraid of the threats from other countries, nor to be terrorized. "**Yahweh Sabaoth is who you must respect as Holy.**" (Is. 8:13) "Wrap up the covenant. Seal the law among **my disciples.**" (Is. 8:14)

The light shines forth, and she has brought forth and delivered a child, a Savior in the time of harvest. "For **a child is born to us.** A son is given to us; and the government will be on his shoulders. **His name will be called Wonderful, Counselor, Mighty God, Everlasting Father, Prince of Peace.** Of the increase of his government and of peace there shall be no end, on David's throne, and on his kingdom, to establish it, and to uphold it with justice and with righteousness from that time on, even forever. The zeal of Yahweh Sabaoth will perform this." (Is. 9:6-7)

Just in this statement by Isaiah shows the time of the year, the autumn of his birth, and is referred to Everlasting Father. The first day of Autumn is September 25th, the harvesting of Apples and Pomegranates, same as referenced in the Song of Songs.

The birth stone which symbolizes the month of September is a Sapphire which also represents the time of the Savior's birth.

For Isaiah even to write, "Everlasting Father," is also referencing to the name of Amen. For the Hebrew prayer opening to this prayer is, "Amen Our Father." The first two letters of Amen is "AM", as in "I AM". The first three letters of Yahweh is "Yah", and in Hebrew "Yah" means, "I AM." So the beginning line of the Hebrew prayer is:

"Amen our Father who art in Heaven, Holy is thy name."

Even the Royal lineage of our Savior, the upright one, represented by name of Yashar'El, our Immanuel is also related by Isaiah. "A shoot will come out of the stock of Jesse, and a branch out of his roots will bear fruit. Yahweh's Spirit will rest on him; the spirit of wisdom and understanding, the spirit of counsel and might, the spirit of knowledge and the fear of Yahweh." (Is. 11:1-2) Even Solomon stated that God himself would live among men.

Yahweh himself came to earth in the time of David and Solomon in which to lead his flock away from sin in order to save the souls of those he loves. Isaiah's writings, not only, shows the Royal lineage, the actual year in history, but the actual month and date in which he was born. That lineage was further explained by Isaiah when he made references to the wolf, the lion, which points to the sons of Jacob.

For the Lion and choice vines and blood of the grapes, a scepter is Judah.

Benjamin is the Wolf, Issachar is the tents, and Zebulon dwells by the sea.

Asher is Royal, and Naphtali bears fawns, and Gad is a lioness. Dan is a lions cub out of Bashan, and Joseph a fruitful vine from there a shepherd. (Det. 33:1-26; Gen. 49:13, 27)

"A star will come out of Jacob, a scepter will rise out of Israel." (Num. 24:17)

"A throne will be established in loving kindness. One will sit on it in truth, in the tent of David, judging seeking justice, and swift to do righteousness." (Is. 16:5)

Our Savior, Our **Immanuel** was also referenced as the **righteous one, which refers to Yashar, in the Book of the Just. "There is no one like God, Jeshurun, who rides on the heavens for your help, in his excellency on the skies." (Det. 33:26)**

Jeshurun is also spelled as Yasharun, which also gives confirmation to what Solomon had said about God living among men. For Yahweh himself came and was born on earth to save his flock, the children that he loves. Yahweh wanted to have them turn from evil, to save their souls from death, and to give them eternal life through him.

"He will destroy in this mountain the surface of the covering that covers all peoples, and the veil that is spread over all nations. **He has swallowed up death forever!** The Lord Yahweh will wipe away tears from off all faces." (Is. 25:7-8)

"It shall be said in that day, "**Behold, this is our God!** We have waited for him, and he **will save us! This is Yahweh! We have waited for him**. We will be glad and rejoice in **his salvation.**! (Is. 25:9)

There is only one true God, one true savior and that is Yahweh. "I myself am Yahweh, besides me, there is no savior." (Is. 43:11) Even the very first Commandment states his name of Yahweh our God, and that we are not to have any gods before him. He is our judge, our Redeemer, our lawgiver, our Savior and King. "I am Yahweh.

That is my name. I will not give my glory to another, nor my praise to engraved images." (Is. 42:8) This also states that Yahweh is his proper name.

During this time period of Isaiah starting from 843 BCE was announcing the birth of our Savior, our Immanuel, the righteous one Yashar'El. That in those days a light will arise dispelling the darkness in the land. Many will come to your light bringing gifts for the King. They will come from Sheba with gold and frankincense, and camels will cover the land from Midian and Ephah, and flocks from Kedar, rams from Nebaioth. They will bring from Lebanon cypress tree, pine and fox trees to beautify the sanctuary. (Is. 60:1-13)

These reference to the trees brought from Lebanon is when David had ordered materials to come for the building of the Temple of Yahweh in Jerusalem. David's son Solomon started to build the Temple, and took seven years to its completion. Which also points to the date of our Savior's birth.

"Then you will know that I, Yahweh, am your Savior, your Redeemer, the mighty one of Jacob." (Is. 60:16) The walls of Jerusalem will be Salvation and the gates Praise. "...but Yahweh will be your everlasting light, and your God will be your glory. Your sun will not go down any more, nor will your moon withdraw itself; for Yahweh will be your everlasting light, and the days of your mourning will end." (Is. 60:18-20)

At this time it will be called Hephzibah, and the land Beulah. In Hebrew the word, "Hephzibah," means "my delight," and "Beulah" which means wedded. (Is. 62:4, 2nd Kgs. 21:1)

Yahweh came to earth himself out of love. "For he said, "Surely, they are my people, children who will not deal falsely, so be became their Savior. In all their affliction he was afflicted, and the angel of his presence saved them. In his love and in his pity he redeemed them. He bore them, and carried them all the days of old." (Is. 63:8-9)

His ancient name was Elyon, and Shadai, and referred to as our Redeemer, and our Father. Even the children of Israel referred to him as Our Father. Even in Psalms 132:7, and in the Book of Isaiah as Heaven his throne, and earth is his footstool. (Is. 66:1)

"Sit at my right hand until I make your enemies a footstool for your feet." (Ps. 110:1)

Another verification of the actual date in antiquities as to the birth of our Savior Yahweh.

The past chapters gave, not only the lineage of people, but the time period within antiquities. For it was the great I AM, Amen Yahweh Himself who came to earth born of Mary, who's name is referenced as Immanuel in the Book of Isaiah, to save his children the flock whom he loves.

In Hannah's ancestry is Perez and Zerah who are twins, which made me realize that Hannah had twin daughters one called Mary, and the other Mariah. Mary was chosen as the mother of our Savior who was born in antiquities of the Old Testament. In the Book Isaiah is the Song of Immanuel, the very name associated with her son.

Even in the Book of **Isaiah**, who lived and died within the 8th century was a prophet of Yahweh. He was the son of Amoz and lived during time of **Uzziah, Jotham, Ahaz and Hezekiah**. Within the Book of Isaiah is the sign of the **Immanuel** which in Hebrew means "**with us is God**." (Is. 7:10-14)

The Hebrew Transliteration of **Immanuel** is:

IM = I Am IMMANU   GOD WITH US
MAN = MAN CREATION
U = TENT PEG
EL = GOD

"I drive him like a **peg** into a firm place; he will become a throne of glory for his father's house." (Is. 23) Or in Zechariah "From him will issue **cornerstone** and **tent peg**.' (Zech. 10:4 also Judges 5:26)

The prophecy of the Messiah's birth wasn't for hundreds of years latter, but within Isaiah's life. "For there is a **child born for us,** a son given to us and dominion is laid on his shoulders; and this is **the name they give him**; Wonder, Counselor, **Mighty God, Eternal Father,** Prince of Peace." (Is. 9:5-6)

Just this passage alone shows the present tense by saying a child is born to us, not a future event. The time perimeter and lineage is also confirmed with:

"A shoot springs from the **stock of Jesse**, a scion thrusts from his **roots**: on him the **spirit of Yahweh rests**, a spirit of wisdom and insight, a spirit of counsel and power, a spirit of knowledge and the fear of Yahweh. (The fear of **Yahweh is his breath**.) (Is. 11:1-2)

The reference to **stock of Jesse is with his son David**, and that God **Yahweh came to earth** to fulfill his promise that he made that He would **live among men – Yahweh is his breath.**

"The path of the **upright man is straight**, you smooth the way of the upright. Following the path of your judgments, we hoped in you, **Yahweh, your name**, your memory are all my soul desires." (Is. 26:7-8)

By saying **upright man is straight** is in reference to Yashar'El as referenced also in the books of Samuel with the **Book of the Just** (2nd Samuel 1:18, and in Joshua 13:2), as well as the name of **Jeshurun** also spelled in Hebrew Cepher as **Yasharun.** (ref. Det. 33:26 and Is. 44:1-8)

Hebrew Cepher states also that **the name** means "**I Am He who breathes life**".

CHAPTER EIGHT
THE GREATEST EVENT

In New Testament they say that Joseph was the husband of Mary, and Simeon and Anna the prophetess were present. Hannah, or called Anna has always been known as a prophetess. "Behold, there was a man in Jerusalem whose name was Simeon. This man was righteous and devout, looking for the consolation of Israel, and the Holy Spirit was on him." (Luke 2:25) "There was one Anna, a prophetess, the daughter of Phanuel, of the tribe of Asher (she was of great age, having lived with a husband seven years from her virginity, and she had been a widow for about eighty-four years), who didn't depart from the temple, worshiping with fastings and petitions night and day." (Luke 2:36-37) Hannah's years of widowhood and length married to her husband is inaccurate.

Hannah the wife of Elkanah was of Penuel or spelled Phanuel, of Perez of Asher. David was annointed King by Hannah's son Samuel. Elkanah was next in line to be King, but died during Aramaean invasion during the time of David around 867BCE.

Hannah during the time of David, when her husband and son Samuel died, was about 69 years of age. She lived another 43 years after this to one hundred and twelve years age.

In the lineage chart you will see that **Shimeon, and Elijah were two of the sons of Harim**. So this Shimeon or spelled Simeon, and Hannah or called Anna, who was a widow of Elkanah, were of great age. **Joseph is one of the sons of Asaph of Berechiah**.

Even Solomon, the son of David, in the following passage refers to the time period of birth, and that God himself came to earth.

"**Now therefore, God of Israel,** please **let your word be verified, which you spoke to your servant David my father. But will God in very deed dwell on the earth."** (1st Kgs. 8:26-27)

"This fear of Yahweh is the beginning of wisdom…" (Ps. 111:10)

"**For the upright he shines like a lamp in the dark….**" (Ps. 112:4)

This line saying "upright" refers to Yashar.

"Quake, earth, at the coming of your Master, at the coming of the God of Jacob, who turns rock into pool, flint into fountain." (Ps. 114:7-8)

"It was the stone rejected by the builders that proved to be **the keystone...**" (Ps. 118:22-23)

"Jerusalem restored! The city, one united whole! Here the tribes come up, the tribes of Yahweh." (Ps. 122:3-4) **The city was united as one by King David.**

"For Yahweh has chosen Zion, deserving this to be his home, "Here I will stay for ever, this the home I have chosen...." Here I will make **horn sprout for David here, I will trim a lamp for my anointed**, whose enemies I shall clothe in shame, while his **crown burst into flower.**" (Ps. 132: 13-18)

"Righteous in all that he does, Yahweh acts only out of Love...." (Ps. 145:17)

The books of New Testament contains some factual information which were excerpts from Old Testament with the books of the prophets which could further substantiate the truth were either lost, or deliberately destroyed by evil.

However, in the book of (Luke 10:38-39) is reference to Martha, "She had a sister called **Mary..**" **Lazarus was their brother and lived with Mary and Martha in Bethany.**

"There was a man named Lazarus who lived in Bethany with **two sisters Mary and Martha,** and he was ill. - It was the **same Mary....**" (John 11:1-2) They sent word to the Messiah, the son of Mary, and he came to them from Jerusalem. "...Martha and Mary to sympathize with them over their brother." (John 11:20) The maiden of Mary called **Rhoda** was referencing to **her daughter?** (.Acts 12:14) **Rhoda means Rose,** and Mary is the Rose of Sharon from the Lily called Hannah, the Spirit of Grace, meaning the child of Hannah her mother. The name Lazarus is a Greek spelling of the name Eliezar, and Mary and Martha are English spellings of the Hebrew names Miriam, and Mariah. Martha was a variant of Roman spelling of Marta. These people lived in antiquities, but in New Testament different names were ascribed to them.

"One of the Levites, the scribe Shemaiah son of Nethanel, recorded them in presence of the King, his officers, Zadok the priest, Ahimelech son of Abiathar..." (1st Chrn. 24:5-8) They drew lots for each family of the sons of Eleazar and for the sons of Ithamar..." (1st Chrn. 24:9) "The first lot fell to **Jehoiarib, to Jedaiah** the second... **Abijah** the eighth, **Jeshua** the ninth..." (1st Chrn. 24:10-11)

"These were the men as registered by their various duties, to enter the Temple of Yahweh, in conformity to their rule handed on by Aaron their father as Yahweh, the God of Israel, had laid it down for him." (1st Chrn. 24:19)

"The sons of Hebron: Jeriah the first, Amariah the second, Johaziel, the third, Jekameam the fourth. **Sons of Uzziel: Micah;** the sons of Micah: Shamir; **the brother of Micah: Isshiah;** for the **sons of Micah: Isshiah, Zechariah.**" (1st Chrn. 24:22-25)

The Cantors:

"For the sons of Asaph; Zaccur, **Joseph,** Nethaniah, Ashareiah." (1st Chrn. 25:2)

"For Heman: **sons of Heman:** Bukkiah, **Mattaniah, Uzziel,** Shebuel, Jerimoth, Hananiah, Hanani..." (1st Chrn. 25:4)

The Levites then appointed **Heman son of Joel, Asaph son of Berechiah, one of his brothers, Ethan** son of Kushaiah, and with them, next in rank, their kinsmen; **Zechariah,** Ben, Jaaziel.... Eliah, Benaiah, Maaseiah, Mattithiah doorkeepers. (1st Chrn. 15:17-18)

Heman, Asaph, and Ethan, the cantors. **Zechariah... Banaiah** were to play the keyed harp. (1st Chrn. 15:19-21)

"**Berechiah and Elkanah** were **doorkeepers of the Ark.**" (1st Chrn. 15:23-24)

David appointed some of the **Levites as ministers before the Ark of Yahweh,** to commemorate, glorify, and praise Yahweh, the God of Israel: first **Asaph,** second **Zechariah,** Mattithiah, Benaiah, Obed-Edom. (1st Chrn. 16:4-5) David put Ark in the Tent.

Tree of Life
May 28, 2007 Artist Karen Sobek
Great I AM Amen, Yahweh came to earth Himself
was born on earth, Our Immanuel, Our Savior
"Hope deferred makes the heart sick, desire fulfilled is a tree of life." Prov. 13:12

The greatest event was with the birth of our **Savior Yahweh**, our **Messiah Yashar'El** on earth. "When that day comes, there will be no more cold, no more frost. It will be a day of wonder-Yahweh knows it – with no alteration of day and night; in the evening it will be light. When that day comes, running waters will issue from Jerusalem, half of them to the eastern sea, half of them to the western sea; they will flow summer and winter. And Yahweh will be King of the whole world. When that comes, **Yahweh will be unique and his name unique.**" (Zech. 14:5-10) **Immanuel, our Yashar'El, our Savior and King.**

"...Jerusalem will go up year by year to worship the **King, Yahweh Sabaoth**, and to keep the **Feast of Tabernacles.**" (Zech. 14:16-18)

The upright one is Yashar'El, **Yahweh our Savior** who came to earth and was born in antiquities in the month and day of **September 25th, the first day of Autumn, Feast of Tabernacles.**

"I will set your stones on carbuncles and your foundations on Sapphires.." (Is. 54:13)

Again the name of **Jeshurun** also spelled in Hebrew Cepher as **Yasharun.** (Det. 33:26 and Is. 44:1-8)

Hebrew Cepher states also that **the name** means, "**I Am He who breathes life**". The Hebrew transliteration of the name is as follows:

> YAH = I AM, I AM AMEN
> SHA = SAVES
> RESH = THE FIRST/CHOSEN ONE
> EL = GOD
> NUN = SEED/KINGSHIP

"...THERE WAS A KING IN JESHURUN.." (DET. 33:5)

I know its hard to keep reading lineages of people, but it shows who was there at the time perimeter of the birth of Our Savior. I have highlighted names for convenience to make you understand the importance of the timeline of people in history, and who was married to Mary and her sister Mariah.

When David called for **Zadok** and the priests and Levites he named them as **Uriel, Asaiah, Joel, Shemiah, Eliel, and Amminadab.** (1st Chrn. 15:11)

"So, the Levites appointed Heman the son of Joel; and of his brothers, Asaph the son of Berechiah; and of the sons of Merari their brothers, Ethan the son of Kushaiah; and with them their brothers of the second rank, **Zechariah**, Ben, Jaaziel, Shemiramoth, Jehiel, Unni, Eliah, Benaiah, **Maaseiah, Mattithiah**, Eliphelehu, Mikneiah, **Obed-Edom,** and Jeiel, **the doorkeepers.**" (1st Chrn. 15:17-18)

Jeshua father of Joiakim, Joiakim father of Eliashib and his son Joiada, and his son Jonathan. (Neh. 12:10-11) **Mattathias son of John, grandson of Simeon.** (1st Macc. 2:1) **Jacob son Simeon** had sons: Nemuel,

Jamin, Jarib, Zerah, Shaul; Shallum his son Mibsam his son, Mishma his son. **The sons of Mishma: Hammuel his son, Zaccur his son, Shimei his son.** (1st Chrn. 4:24-26)

The son of Shimei is Mattathias, son of John, son of Simeon, son of Joiarib. (Neh. 11:10, (1st Chrn. 23:9) The sons of **Joel: Shemaiah and Shimei.** (1st Chrn. 5:8)

Mattathias son is Maath, son Elsi, **Nahum (the prophet),** son Amos who's son is Isaiah, (Luke 3:26) These are the **sons of Heman: Bukkiah, Mattaniah, Uzziel, Shebuel, Jerimoth, Hananiah..**(1st Chrn. 25:7)

Sons of Asaph are Joseph, and Mattathias, or spelled Mattathiah. (1st Chrn 25:2)

David's and captains of army sons of Asaph and of Heman. Sons of Asaph: Zaccur, Joseph, Nethaniah and Asarelah. Joseph the husband of Mary. (1st Chrn. 25:2)

Shimea is also the brother of King David.

Sons of Kohath: **Heman was also the grandson of Samuel and son of Joel of Samuel.** (1st Chrn. 6:19)

"The Levites then appointed **Heman son of Joel, Asaph son of Berechiah, one of his brothers Ethan...**" (1st Chrn. 15:17)

Sons of Kore of the sons of Asaph – Meshelemiah, son of Kore, his son **Zechariah.** (1st Chrn. 26:1-2) Adaiah, and **Zechariah sons of Jeroham.** (2 Chrn. 23:1-3, Neh. 11:4-17)

The following made a covenant and wrote on it the princes, Levites and Priest and sealed it:

Nehemiah son of Hacaliah and Zedekiah, Seraiah, **Azariah**, Jeremiah, Pashhur, **Amariah, Malchijah**, Hattush, Shebaniah, Malluch, **Harim**, Meremoth, **Obadiah, Daniel**, Ginnethon, Baruch, Meshullam, Abijah, **Mijamin**, Maaziah, Bilgai and Shemaiah all priests.

The Levites..Jeshua son of Azaniah, **Mica**....

The chiefs of people....**Adonijah...Hezekiah...**Anathoth...Meshullam. **Zadok, Jaddua.. Anaiah, Hoshea, Hananiah...Shobek...Harim and Baanah.** (Neh. 10:1-27)

These are the people who went with **Zerubbabel son of Shealtiel and Jeshua: Seraiah, Jeremiah, Ezra, Amariah**, Malluch, Hattush, Shecaniah, Rehum, Meremoth, **Iddo**, Ginnethoi, **Abijah, Mijamin**, Maadiah, Bilgah, Shemaiah and **Joiarib**, Jedaiah, Sallu, Antok, **Hilkiah and Jedaiah.** These were chief priests days of Jeshua. (Neh. 12:1-7)

The Levites: Jeshua, Binnui, Kadmiel, Sherebiah, Judah and **Mattaniah.** (Neh. 12:8)

Jeshua father of Joiakim, Joiakim father of Eliashib and his son Joiada and son Johnathan. (Neh. 12:10-11)

Days of Joiakim – Seraiah, Meraiah, **Jeremiah**, Hananiah of Ezra, Meshullam; of **Amariah**, Jehohanan; of Malluchi, Jonathan; of Shebaniah, **Joseph; of Harim**, Adna; of Meraioth, Helkai; of **Iddo**, Zechariah; of Ginnethon, Meshullam; of Abijah, **Zichri**; of Miniamin, of Moadiah, Piltai; of Bilgah, Shammua; of Shemaiah, Johonathan; and **Joiarib**, Mattenai; of Jedaiah, Uzzi; of Sallai, Kallai; Amok, Eber; of Hilkiah, Hosheiah; Jediah, **Nethanel.** (Neh. 12:12-21)

All of this further establishes the time perimeter of when Elkanah and Hannah, and their children lived which was within antiquities, not in the common era.

The books of the Prophets supports the history of the events, and especially with the Book of Isaiah and the Song of Immanuel. And one of the most beautiful songs is the Song of Songs. Even when the Psalms were written by the sons of Korah, as well as, David and Solomon, establishes the time period of the birth of our Savior.

In Psalm 89 by Ethan, The Ezrahite, and of sons of Perez some of the sentences are: (2) "I indeed declare, "Love stands firm forever...." (20) "I have found David, my servant. I have anointed him with my holy oil." (26) "He will call to me, 'You are my Father, my God, and my rock of my salvation!" (27) "I will also appoint him my first-born, the highest of the Kings of the earth."

The Messiah's birth wasn't at the turn of the century, but actually occurred in antiquities as stated in the Book of Isaiah. Even in the Book of **Zechariah** who was a prophet, and the son of **Berechiah, son of Iddo**, stated that **Yahweh** had said, "Daughter of Zion; for **I am coming to dwell in the middle of you – it is Yahweh who speaks.**" (Zech. 2:4)

"Before Zerubbabel be a plain! He will pull out the **keystone...**" (Zech. 4:7) "See now, your king comes to you; he is victorious, he is triumphant, humble and riding on a donkey, on a colt, the foal of a donkey." (Zech. 9:9) To confirm also what was stated by Solomon about God living among men was "...the **House of David will be like God** (like the angel of Yahweh) at their head." (Zech. 12:8, and 1ˢᵗ Kgs. 8:26-27)

"....in the **days of Uzziah King of Judah. Yahweh your God will come....**" (Zech. 14:5)

"And Yahweh will be king of the whole world. When that day comes, **Yahweh will be unique and his name unique.**" (Zech. 14:9-10)

In New Testament it stated that Zechariah and his wife Elizabeth were of great age, who's son is John, and are cousins to Mary. I cannot establish that Elizabeth was his wife, however, she was the daughter of Amminidab, and wife to Aaron. In the lineage chart it does make Zechariah a relative to Hannah and Elkanah, and their daughters Mariah and Mary, who was to give birth to the Messiah, Immanuel, the upright one called Yashar'El.

"Jeshurun whom I have chosen." (Is. 44:2) "One man will say, "I belong to Yahweh," another will call himself by Jacob's name, on his hand another will write, "Yahweh" and be surnamed Israel." (Is. 44:5 see also Det. 33:26) The references in Book of Joshua, and **Book of Samuel to the Upright One, Book of Just, is referring to the Book of Yashar. So Immanuel means God is with us, and Yashar'El means I Am one who saves, the first chosen one called Yahweh. Yah means I AM, which is I AM Amen, Yahweh.**

Our Messiah was born in antiquities, and in the Book of Psalms, "**Yahweh's oracle to you, my Lord, "Sit at my right hand and I will make your enemies a footstool for you.**"

(Ps. 110:1) Even in Psalms 99 "Let us extol Yahweh our God, and worship at his footstool, Holy is He!"

So even in other Psalm the Lord sits at the right hand of King David. "For the **upright** he shines like **a lamp in the dark...**" (Ps. 112:4)

"With you alone is God, and he has no rival; there is no other God, "Truly, **God is hidden with you, the God of Israel, the Savior.**" (Is. 45:14-15)

The reference to the upright is referring to the Book of the Just, Yashar or spelled Jeshar. Even within Deuteronomy refers to God of Jeshurun who rides the heavens. (Det. 33:26)

In Psalm 45 – "The Chief Musician set it to "The Lilies" a contemplation by the sons of Korah. A wedding Song.

(1) My heart overflows with a noble theme. I recite my verses for the king. My tongue is like the pen of a skillful writer.

(2) You are the most excellent of the sons of men. Grace has anointed your lips, therefore God has blessed you forever.

(8) All your garments smell like myrrh, aloes, and cassia. Out of ivory palaces stringed instruments have made you glad.

(9) Kings daughters are among your honorable women. At your right hand the Queen stands in gold of Ophir

(13) The princess inside is all glorious. Her clothing is interwoven with gold.

(14) She shall be led to the king in embroidered work. The virgins, her companions who follow her, shall be brought to you.

(17) I will make your name to be remembered in all generations. Therefore the peoples shall give you thanks forever and ever.

Hannah the mother of Mary was known as the Lily of the Valley.

In Hebrew the spelling of **Hannah meaning Lily, or Rose, and is also spelled Channah meaning Grace, as in the Spirit of Grace, or the children of Grace.**

"I am the rose of Sharon, the **lily of the valleys**. - As a lily among the thistles, so is my love among maidens. - As an apple tree among the trees of the orchard, so is my Beloved among the young men." (The Song of Songs 2:1-3)

Even in the Book of Tobit, "A bright light shall shine over all the regions of the earth; many nations shall come from far away, from all the ends of the earth, to dwell close to the Holy name of the Lord God with gifts in their hands for the King of Heaven. **Within you, generations after generation shall proclaim** their joy, and the **name of her who is Elect** shall endure through the generations to come." (Tobit 13:11-12 webc)

The **gates of Jerusalem shall be built of Sapphire and of Emerald**..." (Tobit 13:21webc) Tobit also stated that he was glad that one of line of his family was so Bless through Tobiel his father, son of **Hananiel**, son of Aduel, son of Abael, son of Raphael, son of Raguel, of **Asiel of the tribe of Naphtali.** (Tobit 1:1 webc)

CHAPTER NINE

JEREMIAH

Jeremiah was the son of Hilkiah, and was only a toddler when Yahweh called upon him to be a prophet. "Behold, I don't know how to speak; for I am a child." (Jer. 1:6)

He was also called the crying prophet from the town of Anathoth. (Jer. 29:27)

It was in this town that people were plotting against Jeremiah for they couldn't accept what he said about stopping their sacrifices to Moloch. (Jer. 11:21-23)

This was during the **dates at least from 870-782 BCE** perimeter of King David with Uzziah, Isaiah, Jeremiah, Ezekiel, Hezekiah, Hilkiah, Joash all being in this time frame.

Another point I want to make is that there were at least nine different Jeremiah's in Old Testament. There is Jeremiah the father of Hamutal. (Jer. 32:1) Another mention as head of Manasseh tribe. (1st Chrn. 5:23-24) A Benjamite that joined with David. (1st Chrn. 12:4) Jeremiah a Gadite. (1st Chrn. 12:10) One of the priests that sealed the Covenant (Neh. 10:2) And was with Zerrubabble (Neh. 12:1, 34) Even in other texts Jeremiah's name is Jeremiah Eleazar. (1st Kgs. 2:26) This is just a few of the examples of different references to Jeremiah.

It states that Jeremiah was son of Hilkiah. Hezekiah and Hilkiah, Joash were in David's administration. King David nominated the cantors as son of Kohath: Heman son of Joel, of Samuel of Elkanah of Azariah, son of Zephaniah. His brother Asaph son of Berechiah. Sons of Merari of Levi: Ethan sons of Amaziah son of Hilkiah of Mushi of Merari. (1st Chrn. 6:16-31) The junior cantors being sons of Asaph, Joseph; for Heman it was Bukkiah, Mattaniah, and Uzziel. (1st Chrn. 25:2-22) David's military and commissioners were: Obadiah son of Shemaiah, Hoshea son of Amaziah, Joel son of Pedaiah and Iddo son of Zechariah.

(1st Chrn. 27:5, 18, 19-21, 32) Elijah son of Jeroham. (1st Chrn. 6:16-31) Isaiah son of Amoz (Is. 1:1) were all in years spanning **870 BCE to 837 BCE, and from 837 BCE to 782 BCE.** Which puts Jeremiah within this time perimeter.

Jeremiah the son of Hilkiah, Hezekiah were from Anathoth. There is also a reference to Jeremiah being a Benjamite that joined with David. (1st Chrn.12:4)

The reference to the town Anathoth itself is a territory belonging to Benjamin which is north of Jerusalem. **Jeremiah the Anathothite at time of King David.** (1ˢᵗ Chrn.12:4)

During this same time period is Uzziah, Zechariah, Elijah, Daniel, Absalom, Hezekiah, and Hilkiah, Jeremiah, Isaiah, Ezekiel and others.

In the Book of Maccabees relates the story of the mother and the **martyr of seven sons which is Jeremiah's mother.** (Jer. 15:1) And the same story is related in Book of Maccabees.

(2ⁿᵈ Macc. 15:15, 36) "She who has borne seven languishes. She has given up the spirit. Her sun has gone down while it was yet day." (Jer. 15:9) **Woe is me, my mother,** that you have borne me, a man of strife, and a man of contention to the whole earth! I have not lent, neither have men lent to me; yet every one of them curses me." (Jer. 15:10)

Jeremiah was of the line of Eleazar. For the reference to be in the Book of Maccabees puts them with David, Daniel, Absalom in dates of **at least 843 BCE-782 BCE.** Also related in Maccabees is **Eleazar** who died a martyr under Antiochus IV because he refused to eat pig that would violate the Laws. (2ⁿᵈ Macc. 6:18-31 webc) In Maccabees, Onias addresses the people say this is the **prophet Jeremiah** who prays for the people. Jeremiah gave Judas Maccabees the sword which was a gift from God. (2ⁿᵈ Macc 15:14-24 webc) It was also Jeremiah when Jerusalem was under siege took the Ark of the Covenant and hid it. When they threw Jeremiah into the well it was Zedekiah who ordered to have him be pulled out. Most people forget that Zedekiah wasn't his original name, but was Mattaniah. (Jer. 34:7, 2ⁿᵈ Kgs. 24:17, Ez. 17)

This corroborates the timeline in history, for Mattaniah was the son of Josiah. Mattaniah is also a Levite singer and the son of Asaph. (2ⁿᵈ Kgs. 24:17 1ˢᵗ Chrn. 20:14) Eleazar son was Phinehas, a grandson of Aaron. (Ex. 6:25) Eleazar was a priest and lawyer descendant of Aaron, son of Phineas. (4ᵗʰ Macc. 7:11-12, 5:4 webc) **Eleazar of Abinadab son of Asap**h who was the **son of Iddo. Shemei son Berechiah his son is Asaph.** So being the son of Hilkiah would put Jeremiah in the line of Eleazar, but not his father. However, why did Jeremiah call Eleazar's wife, his mother, if Eleazar wasn't his father? So Jeremiah is referencing a lineage of his father.

Seraiah was one of the **sons of Uzziah,** and his **son was Asiel** with his **son Asaiah,** and his son being **Tobit.** During this time **Asaiah went with Hilkiah, the son of Shallum, to see the prophetess Huldah the wife of Shallum. Zadok** is the father of Shallum, with Zadok being the son **of Ahitub** in the **line of Zerubabble who is one of the sons of Pedaiah.** Pedaiah sons were Zerubabble, **Shimei,** Joel, and Parosh with Parosh sons being Mijamin and his son **Eleazar. These are sons of Asaph and his son Abinadab.** (Neh. 3:25, 2ⁿᵈ Kg. 25:38, 1ˢᵗ Chrn. 27:20, 3:19)

Mattathias son of John, son of **Simeon priest of sons of Joarib.** (1ˢᵗ Macc. 2:1 webc) and **son of Absalom** (1ˢᵗ Macc. 11:70 webc, 2ⁿᵈ Sam.) Mattithias had five sons John, Simon, Judas and **Eleazar, Jonathan.** (1ˢᵗ Macc. 2:3-6 webc) Absalom's daughter Tamar (Maacah) had sons: Abijah, Attai, Ziza, Shelomith. (2ⁿᵈ Chrn. 11:18-20)

Joarib or spelled Jehoiarib (1ˢᵗ Chrn. 24:7) Of the **priests in Jerusalem: Jedaiah, Jehoiarib,** Jachin, **Azariah son of Hilkiah,** son of Meshullam, son of **Zadok,** son of Meraioth, son of Ahitub, ruler of the House of God." (1ˢᵗ Chrn. 9:10-12) **Phinehas son of Eleazar, Zachariah time of David before he became King.** (1ˢᵗ Chrn.

9:20-21) **Mattathias son of John of Joiarib.** (Neh. 12:11) One of the priests in time of Mattaniah (Zedekiah) and Jeremiah. **Zephaniah the son of Maaseiah, one of the sons of Harim.** (Jer. 37:3)

During the time of **Baruch** the son of Neriah, who wrote all the words on a scroll which Jeremiah dictated the warning words from Yahweh, and read aloud all the warning words to Gemariah, son of Shaphan the secretary. "All the officials were in session there: Elishama the secretary, **Delaiah son of Shemaiah,** Elnathan son of Achbor, Gemariah son of Shaphan, Zedekiah son of Hananiah and all the other officials." (Jer. 36:12-13) Just in this reference shows, not only **Zedekiah of Hananiah** who was one of the sons **of Zerubabble,** but also **Delaiah who with Ezekiel is of the line of Levi.** (see 1ˢᵗ Chrn. 24:16-18, Jer. 36:12))

Of the sons **of Harim is Masseiah** who's sons are **Zephaniah and Neriah.** Neriah son of **Baruch.** (Jer. 21:10, 32:12, 36:4, Ezra 10:20-43) **Nathan of David,** Nahum son **Amos.** (2ⁿᵈ Samuel 5:14,1ˢᵗ Chrn.3:5,14:4)

In the Aprocrypha of Jeremiah, and Coptic versions, it states that **Jeremiah spoke to Pashur. Pashur is the son of Malchijah, of Harim and is the father of Zechariah.**

In the Book of Jeremiah it also states that **he went to Pashur.** (Jer. 20:3, 5)

The Apocrypha are Jewish books called in Greek the Septuagint, and are apart of the cannon of Catholic and Orthodox churches. The Pseudepigrapha is Greek writings that can not be attributed to the author of the book. So in both the Apocrypha, and Torah references Pashur to that time period.

With all the people involved puts them in the span of years from 870 BCE to 782 BCE. For Jeremiah to state that in **those days the House of Judah will unite with House of Israel** could only be under the reign of King David. For it was David when he became King united them as one whole nation. (Jer. 3:18) This also confirms that Jeremiah with Hilkiah and Hezekiah were in that date range.

The incursions from the north when David was battling the Philistines during this **time was Dodo son of Joash,** and Aramaeans, Moabites for Jerusalem. This was one of the first deportations that took place, and when Daniel the son of David was deported to Babylon. It was also the time of Maccabean Rebellion. (1ˢᵗ Chrn. 9:1-34, 14:1-16, 18:1, 2ⁿᵈ Samuel 5:1-25, 2ⁿᵈ Samuel 18:17, 8:10)

Not all people were deported for there still was a remnant remaining in Jerusalem. **Joash** was also Commissioner of cattle for King David, and the keeper of the cellars of oil. (1ˢᵗ Chrn. 27:28-29

Mattathias was the father of the Maccabees, and was of the son of **Shimei, of John, son of Simeon, son of Joiarib.** (1ˢᵗ Chrn. 25:3, Neh. 11:10, 12:11) In the Book of Maccabees it stated that Mattathias was the son of Absalom, and John being of Simeon. (1ˢᵗ Macc.11:70, 2:1-6) **John is the son of Joiarib,** of Athaiah, **of Uzziah the son of Zechariah. Jonathan was the son of Uzziah,** but was also **David's uncle.** (1ˢᵗ Chrn. 27:32, 27:25) Uzziah was also the son of Zechariah of Jeroham. **Absalom was both uncle and father-in-law to Jonathan.**

In Jewish history Cleopas is the surname of Simeon. In New Testament the name Cleopas was being referred to Martha's husband, when it was either Shimeon one of Harims sons, or Mattithias grandson of Absalom.

Mattathias or spelled Mattathiah was known as a doctor. (1st Chrn. 9:30, 1st Macc. 2 webc) And Joiarib was known as a teacher. (Ez. 8:16) **Zechariah or known as Azariah** was the son of Jeroham.

In Hebrew **Mattathias** is Antigonus, and the son of Aristobulus II. And **Aristobolus** is the **grandson of Maccabeus and Absalom.** Absalom is both uncle and father-in-law to Aristobolus. In Hebrew **Aristobolus means Jonathan.** Judas son of Chalphi. (1st Macc. 11:70) Judas was also the son of Hezekiah, and Hezekiah son of Ahaz, married Zechariah's daughter. In Book of Maccabees it listed he had five sons. John is the son of Joiarib. Simon is the son of Onias the son of Jaddua, but also known as the son of Mattithias. Eleazar is the son of Onias, and the brother to Simon. Jonathan is the brother of Judas. Jonathan is also the son of Uzziah. (1st Chrn. 27:25) Shallum son is Mattithiah. (1st Chrn. 9:30, 25:3)

King David's father was Jesse of the sons of Amminadab, of Ram of Hezron, of Korah, of Perez. Amminadab son Korah, of Assir, son Uriel, son **Uzziah,** and sons to Toah, Eliel, sons **of Jeroham.** Asaph's son is Abinadab, and his son was **Eleazar.** (1st Samuel 7:1-2)

The sons of Jeroham are: Asaph, Heman, Elkanah, Zichri, Adaiah and Zechariah (Azariah), and Elijah. David's father Jesse lineage is also of Jeroham.

Of Libni his sons are **Joah** and **Iddo.** Shemei's son **Berechiah** with his son being **Asaph,** and his son being **Abinadab,** and he was one of the **sons of Jesse father of David.**

So Mattithias is the son of Asaph son of Berechiah of the line of Absalom of David. Of the sons of Merari was **Shimei, his son Ethan, Zechariah and Mattathiah.** (1st Chrn. 6:42, 15:12, 16:5)

Mattathiah is also spelled as Mattathias, and in Hebrew known as Aristobolus.

In Maccabees it stated that Joseph was the son of Zechariah. (1st Macc, 5:17-18) The actual lineage is of the sons of **Asaph: Zaccur, Joseph, Nethaniah** and Asharelah. They were also the captains of the army of King David. (1st Chrn. 25:1-2) Other sons of Asaph of Heman are: **Shimei, Mattithias, Zichri, Joah, Zechariah.** (2nd Chrn. 29:12-14)

In the book of Maccabees lists that Mattathias as being the son of Absalom.

Absalom did have have three sons and one daughter Tamar. (2nd Samuel 14:27) Absalom's daughter was Tamar (Maacah) who had sons: Abijah, Attai, Ziza, Shelomith. (2nd Chrn. 11:20)

Different sources has Jeremiah doing prophecy around 721 BCE, while others state it is 626 BCE. These dates would put him out of the correct alignment in history with the Maccabees, Absalom, and King David. Maccabees cleansed the sanctuary of profanity on same day that it was profaned, and kept celebration for eight days in same manner of Feast of Tabernacles.

For Jeremiah to be listed with the Maccabees puts him along with Hezekiah, and Hilkiah within the timeline of the Maccabean revolt and with King David. So they were all within the date perimeter of the beginning of Maccabean Rebellion **843 BCE to at least 843.3-837 BCE when it ended.** For Jeremiah to be in the Book of

Maccabees along with Mattathias and Absalom, the son of David, coupled with Jeremiah speaking to Pashur, who is one of the sons of Harim, puts him in my correct timeline of history.

The prophets at this time; Isaiah, Jeremiah, Zechariah, and even Ezekiel were all referencing the time period which led to the birth of our Savior, Our Immanuel, Yashar'El.

"See, the days are coming – it is Yahweh who speaks-when I will raise a virtuous Branch for David, who will reign as true King and be wise, practicing honesty and integrity in the land. In his days Judah will be saved and Israel dwell in confidence. And this is the name he will be called Yahweh our Integrity." (Jer. 23:5-6)

CHAPTER TEN

EZEKIEL

The very opening of the Book of Ezekiel states that he was on the river **Chebar.** Chabar in the Paleo-Hebrew, or old Hebrew, that is referenced in ancient Palestine of Judea an area around the Jordan called Chabar where the Nabataeans resided.

But what is of the outmost importance is that people were led into captivity to Tel Aviv that lived by the river Chebar. "Then I came to them of the **captivity at Tel Aviv**, that lived by the river Chebar." (Ezk. 3:15) There are currently today two rivers in Tel Aviv called, Yarkon and Ayalon Rivers. The Judean hills empties into the Yarkon River, and is the closest in proximity to the sea, and empties into the Mediterranean Sea.

The River Ayalon also has its origins from the Judean hills as well, but empties into the Yarkon River. In antiquities the hill, or "tel" refers to the city on the hill by the river Chabar also spelled as Kabar. The Hebrew root meaning of Kabar is abundant, delta or sieve, but also refers to canal.

So in this reference the Chebar is not the one in Babylon, but in Tel Aviv, Israel. Babylon is a landlocked country, meaning it does not reside, or border any ocean. So the reference to Chebar being at Tel Aviv is accurate for in the passage, "He took me to the east. I saw the glory of the God of Israel approaching from the east..A sound came with it, like the **sounds of the ocean**...like the one I had seen on the bank of the river Chebar." (Ezk. 43:2-3)

Ezekiel saw a storm come out of the north like a chariot and gave the description of the wheels which looked like Beryl. The expanse over it looked like a throne, as an appearance of a Sapphire stone with a man above it. This description gives several meanings for the Sapphire stone is associated with the month of September, and the throne is referring to the most high God. God's ancient name was Elyon which is most high, and Yah meaning the great I AM Amen. Even Ezekiel stated, "This was the appearance of the likeness of Yahweh's glory." (Ezk. 1:26) Yahweh is the one true God.

This was the time that Ezekiel was called to eat the scroll in which to prophecy to the House of Israel. The House of Israel occupied the northern part of Israel while Judah occupied the lower southern parts of Israel. This time perimeter was before King David united the kingdom into one whole nation.

Yahweh carried Ezekiel to the people in captivity at **Tel Aviv** by the river Chebar. Ezekiel was to warn them of their wickedness by saying the warning is from Yahweh. "At the end of seven days, Yahweh's word came to me, saying, "Son of man, I have made you a watchman to the house of Israel. Therefore hear the word from my mouth, and warn them from me. When I tell the wicked, 'You will surely die; and you give him no warning, nor speak to warn the wicked from his wicked way, to save his life; that wicked man will die in his iniquity; but I will require his blood at your hand. Yet if you warn the wicked, and he doesn't turn from his wickedness, nor from his wicked way, he will die in his iniquity; but you have delivered your soul." (Ezk. 3:16-19)

In order to try to save the House of Israel, and the House of Judah Ezekiel was to bear their sins. He had to lay on his left side to bear the sins of House of Israel for the number of years sinned in which each year would count as a day. So for the House of Israel he had to lay there for 390 days. Then for the House of Judah he had to lay on his right side for 40 days. Yahweh was trying to have them turn from their wicked ways, but even warned that if they did not turn from wickedness that their land would become a desolation with increased famine and pestilence.

This was one of the first deportations of people to different areas, but yet a remnant remained within Jerusalem.

Ezekiel was carried again from his home in Judah to the door of the inner gate in Jerusalem. This door of the gate of the inner court that looks to the north where abominations by the House of Israel were being done. "He brought me to the door of the court, and when I looked, behold, a hole in the wall. Then he said to me, "Son of man, dig now in the wall." When I had dug in the wall, I saw a door. He said to me, "Go in, and see the wicked abominations that they do here." So I went in and looked, and saw every form of creeping things, abominable animals, and all the idols of the House of Israel, portrayed around on the wall. Seventy men of the elders of the house of Israel stood before them. In the middle of them Jaazaniah the son of Shaphan stood, every man with his censer in his hand, and the smell of the cloud of incense went up." (Ezk. 8:7-11)

Yahweh took Ezekiel to the inner court of Yahweh's house. "He brought me into the inner court of Yahweh's house; and I saw at the door of Yahweh's temple, between the porch and the altar, there were about twenty-five men, with their backs toward Yahweh's temple, and their faces toward the east. They were worshiping the sun toward the east." (Ezk. 8:16)

The reference to them worshiping the sun which has its origins in paganism from Babylonian, Persian and India, and Egyptian pagan cult worship of the sun Ra and Horus his son. Even the Romans called this pagan worship of the sun as being Sol Invictus.

Even Zechariah in the gnostic texts referred to him seeing a man standing in the form of a animal, the ass, inside the Temple, went out and said, "Woe unto you, whom do ye worship?" The person with a ass head referring to the anti-god, and the abominations being done within the Temple. (Lost Books of the Bible)

Yahweh called for a man dressed in linen with a inkhorn to go through Jerusalem and mark a cross on the foreheads of those who despise the abominations being committed. This cross is known as the Jeremiah cross.

"Then he said to me, "The iniquity of the house of Israel and Judah is exceedingly great, and the land is full of blood, and the city full of perversion.." (Ezk. 9:9)

The elder sister is Samaria and the younger sister is Sodom that was filled with such perversion as referenced in chapter 16, shows how perverted it was for Abraham stood, and witnessed the destruction of Sodom. (Gen. 19:20)

Even Moses referred to the destruction of Sodom. (Det. 29:22-23, see Zephaniah 2:9)

The prophets have been warning people to repent, and renounce their sins to gain life instead of being in love with death. "Why are you so anxious to die, House of Israel? I take no pleasure in the death of anyone – it is the Lord Yahweh who speaks.

Repent and live." (Ezk. 18:30-32) Yahweh was warning them through his prophets, not to go into Egypt, and not to worship alien gods, or lust after the Assyrians.

Yahweh never wanted anyone to hurt his people, but he didn't want his children committing sins and worshiping false gods either. He knew that there were some within his people who were evil and did perversions, and tried to lead others into blaspheming against God Yahweh. And yet, God warned the good of the destructive force that was coming from the North, and the siege against Jerusalem. "Ezekiel is to be a sign for you. You are to do just as he has done. And when this happens, you will learn that I Am Yahweh." (Ezk. 24:24)

It was one thing for God their Father to correct his children from going astray, and another thing for an enemy to come against him and his children to inflict such harm simply out of hatred. The enemy of God wanted to inflict such pain upon his people, and to show such hatred for God by profaning of the very Temple of God. The forces which came against them were the Ammornites, Moab, Edom, Philistines, Tyre and Babylon.

"No more, for the House of Israel, shall any of the hostile nations surrounding her be a thorn that wounds or a brier that tears; and so men will learn that I am Lord Yahweh." (Ezk. 28:24) The thorn, or thistle, is Lebanon.

Other writers put Ezekiel in the timeline of 600 BCE when he was prophesying, when it was before David became King. This is established by the passage, "I mean to raise up one shepherd, my servant David, and to put him in charge of them and he will pasture them; and be their shepherd. I, Yahweh, will be their God, and my servant David shall be their ruler." (Ezk. 34:23-24)

This also confirms my own timeline of history. For when David was anointed by Samuel and he became King, it was David who united Israel and Judah into one nation in the year 869-870 BCE.

Another passage in Ezekiel further establishes my timeline with, "I shall make them into one nation in my own land and on the mountains of Israel, and one king is to be king of them all; they will no longer form two nations nor be two separate kingdoms." (Ezk. 37:22-23)

The land of Palestine of Judea was divided before David into two kingdoms of which Israel formed the northern area while Judah remained in the southern section which contained the city of Jerusalem. This was also the beginnings of the siege on Jerusalem, and Yahweh's cleansing of the city from all the perversions and sins being committed. Even the Maccabees during this period of time cleansed the city, and the tabernacle several years latter, on the very same day that the Altar and Tabernacle were profaned.

Also keep in mind that at this period in history it was not the Temple which was destroyed, but the walls and city itself which was left desolate. King David laid the keystone for the Temple with its inscription, but the actual Temple was only built by his son Solomon after his death, and took seven years to complete. It was also Solomon who stated after the Temple was completed that now will God surely live among men on earth which God promised to his father David. Even the Ark of the Covenant, which King David brought to Jerusalem was inscribed, and bears the name of Yahweh who is seated above the cherubs. (1st Chrn. 13:6-7)

All the events that took place was leading to the greatest event in history the birth of Yahweh on earth which Isaiah was stating in the Song of Immanuel. Elijah was proclaiming to make a straight highway for our God across the desert. While Elisha was referring to the Chariots of God. The Chariot of God (Ps. 68:17 and Ezk. 1:4-28) As Ezekiel described the wheels of the chariot. Even in the Book of Jeremiah, "In those days and at that time, I will cause a Branch of righteousness to grow up to David. He will execute justice and righteousness in the land. In those days Judah will be saved, and Jerusalem will dwell in safely. This is the name by which she will be called: Yahweh our righteousness." (Jer. 33:15-16)

During the reign of Solomon they dwelled in peace.

In Psalms David said to the Lord sit at my right hand and I will make you a footstool. (Ps. 99:4-5) Or in Psalm 132:13-18 it states, "For Yahweh has chosen Zion, desiring this to be his home, "Here I will stay forever, this is the home I have chosen. "I will bless her virtuous with riches, provide her poor with food, vest her priests in Salvation and her devout shall shout for joy." Here, I will make a horn sprout for David, here, I will trim a lamp for my anointed, whose enemies I shall clothe in shame, while his crown burst into flower."

David was God's Holy anointed for from David's line was born Our Savior, Our Immanuel, known as the righteous, upright one called Yashar'El.

"With you alone is God, and he has no rival; there is no other God. Truly, God is hidden with you, the God of Israel, the Savior" (Is. 15:14-15)

"As Yahweh has been with my lord the king, so may he be with Solomon and make his throne even greater than the throne of the lord King David." (1st Kgs. 1:37, 2nd Chrn. 6:17-18)

CHAPTER ELEVEN

ZECHARIAH

The very opening of the Book of Zechariah sets the lineage, and time perimeter in history by saying, "Zechariah the son of Berechiah, the son of Iddo, the prophet". Many people always questioned which Berechiah, and which Zechariah was it? There were in fact several Zechariah's within Old Testament, but only one which has that lineage which is of the sons of Merari of Levi. The way the people were written in Old Testament made it very confusing, and it took me along time to unavel this mystery of God. Like the Book of Daniel which has years in 167 BCE doesn't mean that is when Daniel lived, but when the book was written. The same as with the Book of Zechariah for it doesn't mean that Zechariah lived in the days of Darius, 520 BCE, but when the book was written.

The sons of Merari are Libni and Shemei. With the son Shemei who had a son called Berechiah, and his son is Asaph. The son Libni had sons called Joah and Iddo who's son is Asaph, and his son was Abinadab. Asaph is the son of Berechiah, and Asa who was of Abijah of Samuel was also referred to being of Berechiah.

That is the first part of the mystery, however, to further unravel the lineage is to look at the sons of Jeroham. For some of sons of Jeroham are:

Asaph, Heman, Elkanah, Zichri, Adaiah, Zechariah, Elijah.

Of the sons of Asaph are: Mattithias, Zichri, Joah, Zechariah, Joseph, Zaccur, Nethaniah. It is this Zechariah the son of Jeroham which continues the lineage to the birth of Our Immanuel. For this Zechariah had a son called Uzziah, and from him came Athaiah, his son Ahaziah, to Joiarib and his son John, and Jedaiah. Which are some of the people listed even in the Book of Maccabees. The sons of Jeroham puts them in dates of 869 BCE.

The sons of Simeon: Shaul, his son Shallum...Zaccur his son Shimei. (1st Chrn. 4:24-27) Son of Shimei is Mattathias son of John, son of Simeon, son of Joiarib. (Neh. 12:11) The children of Judah, Athaiah, son of Uzziah, son of Zechariah, son of Amariah, son of Shephatiah son of Mahalalel, of children of Perez. The Maaseiah son of Baruch, son of Colhozeh, son of Hazaiah, son of Adaiah, son of Joiarib, son of Zechariah, son of the Shilonite.

All sons of Perez live in Jerusalem. Jedaiah, son of Joiarib Seriah son of Hilkiah of Zadok, and Mattithiah of Levi. (Neh. 11:3-7, 1ˢᵗ Chrn. 6:46-47, 15:8, 25, Neh. 8:4)

Adaiah son of Jeroham, son Pelaliah his son Amzi, son of Zechariah, son of Pashur, son of Malchijah. (Neh. 11:12) Malchijah is one of the sons of Harim of Ethni of the line of Gershom of Levi.

For Zechariah and Elkanah being of the sons of Jeroham makes them brothers, and Elkanah's wife Hannah sister-in-law to Zechariah. But in New Testament they call Mary a cousin of Zechariah when in fact he was her uncle. Zechariah's daughter was named Abijah or Abi for short, and it was Abi who was the mother of Hezekiah. (2ⁿᵈ Kgs. 18:1-3) Isaiah the prophet was also a consultant to Hezekiah.

Remember that within time frame of King David sieges were being done to Jerusalem, and other towns for several years. And according to Zechariah it was being done for past 70 years. King David laid the keystone for the Temple and even put a inscription on it. "For this is the stone which I am placing before Joshua: on this single stone there are seven eyes; and I myself into it put the inscription – it is Yahweh who speaks." (Zech. 3:7) This Keystone was only laid by King David. (Ps. 118:19-22, 1ˢᵗ Chrn. 13:6-7, Jer. 3:15-18, 1ˢᵗ Kgs. 6:37)

It was Zerubabble who pulled out the Keystone and who laid the the foundations for the Temple. (Zech. 4:9) It was Solomon who built the first actual Temple. Pedaiah sons were Zerubbable and Shimei, with his son being Parosh and his son Mijamin and his son Eleazar. Jeshua or called Joshua, Jeshua was also the son of Jozadek. (Ez. 3:8)

These were in Jerusalem at the time of King David.

During the sieges against Jerusalem Yahweh was taking care of his flock in the House of Judah. "From him will issue Cornerstone and Tent Peg from him the bow of battle from him all the leaders." (Zech. 10:3-4) The bow is Judah and the Cornerstone is the Keystone and the tent peg is Our Immanuel.

The Hebrew Transliteration of **Immanuel** is:

IM = I Am IMMANU GOD WITH US
MAN = MAN CREATION
U = TENT PEG
EL = GOD

The Ark of the Covenant was in a Tent which David erected in Jerusalem until the Temple could be built. This all was leading to the birth of Our Immanuel. It was Zerubabble who laid the foundation for the Temple that Solomon built. (Zech. 4:9)

"When that day comes, a fountain will be opened for the House of David and the citizens of Jerusalem, for sin and impurity." (Zech. 13:1) The fountain of life which only comes from Yahweh.

When Our Immanuel was born, and during the time of David, and with Solomon, the country was at peace.

"Judah and Israel lived safely, every man under his vine and under his fig tree, from Dan even to Beersheba, all the days of Solomon." (1st Kgs. 4:25)

"For a child is born to us. A son is given to us; and the government will be on his shoulders. His name will be called Wonderful, Counselor, Mighty God, Everlasting Father, Prince of Peace. Of the increase of his government and of peace there shall be no end, on David's throne and on his kingdom, to establish it, and to uphold it with justice and with righteousness from that time on, even forever. The zeal of Yahweh of Sabaoth will perform this." (Is. 9:6-7) The mention to Our Father is referencing the Great I AM, Amen, Yahweh. For the very beginning of the Hebrew prayer is "Amen Our Father."

"You Yahweh, are Our Father, Our Redeemer from everlasting is your name." (Is. 63:16)

It will happen when the nations will seek the root of Jesse which stands as the banner of Yahweh for peace. "Yahweh Sabaoth says: "In those days, ten men will take hold, out of all the languages of the nations, they will take hold of the skirt of him who is a Jew, saying, 'We will go with you, for we have heard that God is with you.'" (Zech. 8:23)

"Rejoice greatly, daughter of Zion! Shout, daughter of Jerusalem! Behold, your King comes to you! He is righteous, and having salvation; lowly, and riding on a donkey, even on a colt, the foal of a donkey." (Zech. 9:9)

"I myself AM Yahweh, besides me, there is no savior." (Is. 43:11)

"I AM Yahweh, and there is no one else. Besides me, there is no God." (Is. 45:5)

The prophets were all relating to the Greatest Event in the History of the earth the birth of Our Savior, Our Immanuel, the Righteous One. Yahweh himself came to born on earth to save his flock, his people for whom he loves. In Scripture it stated that his name would be unique and the time of day would be unique. Even in the Book of Isaiah referenced to the name of Jeshurun which is also spelled Yasharun. Yashar is the book of The Just mentioned in Books of Joshua and Samuel. Yashar'El is the upright one, the righteous who Elijah called out to people tell them to make the path straight for the upright one.

"....in the **days of Uzziah King of Judah. Yahweh your God will come....**" (Zech. 14;5) "And Yahweh will be king of the whole world. When that day comes, **Yahweh will be unique and his name unique.**" (Zech. 14:9-10) Even Solomon said when he built the Temple, "So now, God of Israel, let the words come true which you spoke to your servant David, my father. Yet will God really live with men on earth?" (1st Kgs. 8:26-27)

To clarify the year in history is to know that Isaiah started prophesying in year 869 BCE and Zechariah and Iddo were in this timeframe. In the days of King David timeframe of 869 BCE, were Obadiah, Hoshea the son of Amaziah, Iddo and Zechariah, Elijah the sons of Jeroham. Also timeframe of 843-837 BCE were **Hosea son of Beeri in the days of Uzziah,** Jotham, Ahaz and Hezekiah. **Uzziah was the son of Zechariah** of Jeroham also known as Azariah, and the Maccabees.

Even though they reference to King of Uzziah doesn't mean that's when his whole life span began, or which Uzziah they referred too, for he lived a life before he became King of Judah. Other texts put Uzziah in year 782 instead of when he resided in Jerusalem in the year of 821 BCE. The King Uzziah referred too, was only 16 years old when he came to the throne. Zechariah didn't write the book others wrote it after the time of Zechariah. So when it was written they referred to King Uzziah, when in fact, it was probably Uzziah son of Zechariah which made him of great age, and living in Jerusalem around 847-837 BCE.

In the book of Haggai it said, "...my spirit remains among you." (Haggai 1:15, 2:4-5)

From the twenty-four day of the ninth month, from the day the foundations of the sanctuary of Yahweh was laid. (Haggai 2:18-19) this puts the timeline 837 BCE.

For the spirit to be among them is to say the He resides among them. Not in a future tense, but in the present tense.

Yahweh brought them out of Egypt and led them into Israel. "Yet I am Yahweh your God from the land of Egypt, and you shall acknowledge no god but me, and besides me there is no savior." (Is. 13:4)

David laid the keystone, and Solomon built the Temple so the foundations were laid about 837 BCE when Zerubabble laid the foundation. It was Zerubabble who laid the foundation for the Temple that Solomon built. (Zech. 4:9) The Temple was completed in seven years at the date of 827 BCE.

"Arise, shine, for your light has come, and Yahweh's glory has risen on you. For, behold, darkness will cover the earth, and thick darkness the peoples; but Yahweh will arise on you, and his glory shall be seen on you. Nations will come to your light, and kings to the brightness of your rising." (Is. 60:1-3)

It took the Maccabees to cleanse the sanctuary of all the profanity committed by the aliens. It was cleansed two years to the day it was profaned to its cleansing. They celebrated for **eight days** as in the Feast of Tabernacles. When coming to the inner court through the gates there are eight steps in which to ascend. (Ezk. 40:28-32)

Eight in the beginning, and eight in the end. A 88 key melody, a Song of Love, from Eternity to Eternity. For the number 8 symbolizes eternity to eternity, and symbolizes the 8th Eternal day.

The Eternal God I AM Amen, Yahweh, the first and the last. "I Am Yahweh, and there is no one else. Besides me, there is no God." (Is. 45:5) "I myself AM Yahweh, besides me, there is no Savior." (Is. 43:11)

Most of the people involved in antiquities led the way to the Greatest Event in history, the birth of Our Savior, Our Immanuel.

See the chart on next page to help further clarify the timeline of events in history.

To clarify that people lived during certain times in antiquities is to show the timeline of history.

870	The Ark of God was brought out of Kiriath-jearim and moved to Obed-Edom for three months. The Ark called by his name of Yahweh. (2nd Samuel 6:2)
	War with Philistines where Saul and sons were killed at Mt. Gilboa
	David battles Philistines, Moabites, Aramaeans, Ammonite for Jerusalem.
	Samuel annoints David King.

879	**Daniel son of David deported to Babylon** (1ˢᵗ Chrn. 9:1-34, 18:1, 2ⁿᵈ Samuel 5:1-25) The Levites were Heman son of Joel, Asaph son of Berechiah, Zechariah, Elkanah, Mattithiah doorkeepers, and Berechiah and Elkanah doorkeepers to the Ark. Priests were Shebaniah, Joshaphat, Nethaniel, Amassi, Zechariah, Benaiah and Eliezer. (1ˢᵗ Chrn. 15:1-24) Levites before the Ark were Asaph, Zechariah and Mattithiah. (1ˢᵗ Chrn. 16:5) Elkanah was next in line to be King, and husband of Hannah, and father of Mary dies during the Aramaean invasion. The children of Hannah & Elkanah were: Samuel, Abijah, Eliezar, Mary and Mariah.
870	Ark being moved to Jerusalem and Philistines attacked again. Uzzah, Ohio, sons of Abinadab drove the cart carrying the Ark. (2ⁿᵈ Samuel 6:3)
870	King David nominated Cantor, of sons of Kohath: **Heman** son of Joel, son of Samuel of Elkanah, of Jeroham. **Azariah**, son of **Zephaniah**. His brother Asaph son of Berechiah. Sons of Merari: Ethan, and sons of Amaziah, son of Hilkiah of Mushi of Merari of Levi..(1ˢᵗ Chrn.6:16-47) The sons of Asaph who are Zaccur, Joseph, Nethaniah, Asharelah. For Heman was Bukkiah, Mattaniah, Uzziel. (1ˢᵗ Chrn.25:1-4) Jeremiah son of Hilkiah (Jer. 1:1) **Jeremiah and Nathan with David.** (Jer.30:9) **Ezekiel of Levi.** **Elijah** son of Jeroham (1ˢᵗ Chrn.8:26-27) **Isaiah** son of Amoz (Is. 1:1, 2ⁿᵈ Chrn. 26:22-23) Shimei; Joah son of Zeruiah, Jehosphahat son of Ahilud, recorder. Zadok of Ahitub, Ahimelech son of Abiathar and Seraiah the scribe. Benaiah son of **Jehoiada.** (2ⁿᵈ Samuel 8:15-18) Of Simeon: Shaul, his son Shallum…Zaccur his son Shimei. (1ˢᵗ Chrn. 4:24-27) Son of Shimei is Mattathias son of John, son of Simeon, son of Joiarib. (Neh. 12:11) King David's military and civilian commissioners were: Banaiah champion of the 30; Elihu one of David's brothers; Obadiah, Ishmaiah, Hoshea son of Amaziah; Joel son of Pedaiah; **Iddo son of Zechariah** and Jonathan David's uncle. (1ˢᵗ Chrn. 27:5, 18, 19-21, 32)

868	War with Hadadezer king of Zobah, Chaldees. Ammonite invasion Jews deported to Babylon. (1st Chrn. 18:1-30, 9:1-2, 2nd Samuel 10:6) Arsaces title of King of Parthia and Media as contained in books of **Isaiah, Jeremiah** and **Maccabees.**
868	Jews placed in Assyia by the Medes (Jer. 2:11, 28) **Zechariah of Berechiah of Iddo** (1st Chrn. 27:21)
843.31	The Maccabean Rebellion with Absalom, Mattathias, Jeremiah mentioned in the book, Eleazar. Maccabees is the Hasmonean revolt against Antiochus who profaned the Sanctuary
843	Famine 3 years (2nd Samuel 21:1)
849	**Isaiah's Song of Immanuel Isaiah** son of Amoz (Is. 1:1, 2nd Chrn. 26:23) **Tobit** (Tobit 13:11-14, 20-23)
840	Another war with Philistines at Gob. Benaiah son of Jehoiada (2nd Sam. 8:15-18)
838	Census done (1st Chrn. 27:24) **Mary and Joseph**
838	Herodotus (Heroides Antipater) the Idumaean dies.
837	Maccabean Rebellion ends (2nd Samuel 20:14-26) Maccabees cleanse abominations in Sanctuary
837	**King David laid the Keystone YHWH September 25th month of Tishri and theFeast of Tabernacles.** People at this time **Zechariah (Azariah) son Uzziah, Nathan, Zadok, Abinadah, and Ahinadab son of Iddo,** and **Shemei.** (1st Kgs. 4:1-19) These even under Solomon's reign where the Priests and Princes that sat under their own vine and **fig tree.**

CHAPTER TWELVE

SUMMARY

Throughout Old Testament God Yahweh, not only, told you his name, but told you that there was no other God but him, and that He was Our Savior, and Our King. Even the First Commandment of God Yahweh stated that you are to have no other gods but him. "I Am Yahweh your God, who brought you out of the land of Egypt, out of the house of bondage. "You shall have no other gods before me." (Det. 5:6)

"I AM Yahweh that is my name. I will not give my glory to another, nor my praise, to engraved images." (Is. 42:8) Even the very Ark of the Covenant is engraved YHWH called by His name of Yahweh. (2nd Samuel 6:2)

The Great I AM is Amen, Yahweh. And the first three letters of Yahweh is "YAH" which means I AM. "... through him also rises the Amen to God unto our glory." (2nd Chrn. 1:20)

In Hebrew the word "ben" means son of. So to say "Ben Israel" references lineage surname, or son of Israel.

"One will say, 'I Am Yahweh's;' and another will be called by the name of Jacob; and another will write with his hand 'to Yahweh,' and honor the name of Israel." (Is. 44:5)

It is also phrased as saying, 'and be surnamed Israel,' or of Israel who is Jacob.

So many people followed the New Testament Gospels, and were mislead into believing that they are of truth when they are forged books to give praise to the Roman Emperors. I do not follow New Testament for many of those books were forged under the reign of Constantine to form his one world religion which was based on pagan ideology of the trinity of gods. Constantine created a mythical logos name of a son called iesus (ieous), or jesus christ, based on Roman sol invictus, which is the worship of the sun god, and his son.

I follow Old Testament for all truth is contained within the Books of the Torah. To follow Old Testament, and the people involved in those events correlates to the true timeline of history. My book is the humble attempt to clarify history to give Glory to the One True God Yahweh, and to the true Holy Family of Hannah and Elkanah. For the Greatest Event in History of the world was the birth of Yahweh on earth in the timeline of antiquities.

He came to earth himself out of love for his flock, for his chosen children, to fight the influence of evil, in which to save their very souls from death.

The correct parents of the Blessed Mother Mary is Hannah and Elkanah. Hannah means Lily, or spelled Channah which means Grace, as in the spirit of Grace, or children of Grace. Chava in Hebrew means Eve, who is the mother of all.

Hannah was the wife of Elkanah, and had three sons and two daughters. The names are: Samuel, Abijah, Eliezar (Lazarus in Greek), Mary and Mariah.

Hannah was a great prophetess from the tribe of Asher, and Elkanah was descendant of Jeroham of Levi of Judah. King David's lineage is of the tribe of Judah. Zechariah also descends from Jeroham which makes him a brother to Elkanah, and uncle to Hannah's children. In Hannah's lineage line there are twins called Perez and Zerah. So Hannah may have given birth to twins, of which the daughters are named Mary and Mariah.

I came to the realization that Hannah had twin daughters, Mary and Mariah, from the Song of Songs, where it referenced, "Your cheeks, behind your veil, are halves of pomegranate. There are sixty queens and eighty concubines and countless maidens. But my dove is unique, mine unique and perfect. She is the darling of her mother, the favorite of the one who bore her. The maidens saw her, and proclaimed her blessed." (Song of Songs 6:6-8)

Hannah and Elkanah were of Royal lineage which makes their children of Royal lineage. Elkanah was actually next in line to become King, but unfortunately died during the Aramaean invasion. It was Hannah's son Samuel who anointed David King and united the people as one nation. This uniting of the nation took place before the birth of Our Savior, Our Immanuel. And it was King David who inscribed the Keystone for the Temple that Solomon would build with tetragammaton of YHWH that stands for the proper name of YAHWEH.

Elijah and Zechariah both of who, like Elkanah, are also the sons of Jeroham.

Some of the sons of Jeroham are: Asaph, Heman, Elkanah, Zichri, Adaiah, Zechariah and Elijah.

It was Elijah who went through the country proclaiming to make the paths straight, a highway for out God. "A voice cries, "prepare in the wilderness a way for Yahweh. Make a straight highway for out God across the desert." (Is. 40:3) In Deuteronomy and Isaiah they referred to Jasharun or spelled as Yasharun, meaning the Upright man who's path is straight.

Zechariah, the brother of Elkanah, was also referred as being the son of Berechiah, the son of Iddo, the prophet. Berechiah and Iddo are of the sons of Merari of Levi. In fact, Berechiah son is Asaph. Asaph's sons are Mattithias, Zichri, Joah, Zechariah, Joseph, Zaccur, Nethaniah. This should give you a good idea of the timeline for Berechiah came before Jeroham in the history of the Bible. Even in the Book of Isaiah references the son of Berechiah, "...Uriah, the priest, and Zechariah the son of Jeberechiah." (Is. 8:2) It was Berechiah and Elkanah who were the gatekeepers to the Ark of God. (1st Chrn. 15:23-24) A son born to Asa was also named Jehosphaphat of Berechiah of Elkanah. Asa was the son of Abijah of Samuel. It was this Joseph, the son of Asaph of Berechiah, who was chosen to be with Mary.

The prophecy of the Messiah's birth was being proclaimed by Isaiah around 849 BCE with the Song of the Immanuel. "Behold, the virgin will conceive, and bear a son, and shall call his name Immanuel." (Is. 7:14)

"For there is a child born for us, a son given to us and dominion is laid on his shoulders; and this is the name they give him; Wonder, Counselor, Mighty God, Eternal Father, Prince of Peace." (Is. 9:5-6) The very name Immanuel means:

IM = I Am Immanu, God with us, Man = man creation, U = Tent Peg, El = God. Zechariah and Isaiah both referred to the words "tent peg," and "cornerstone". It was Zerubabble who pulled out the keystone.

The prophets knew that the Savior would come forth from the stock of Jesse, and that the spirit of Yahweh rests within him. "The fear of Yahweh is his breath." (Is. 1:1-2)

The stock of Jesse is of the lineage of Jesse, and Jesse is the father of King David.

Elkanah, Mary's father, was a prince among the people, which makes Mary and Mariah, princesses. The Blessed Mother Mary was of Royalty not of lowly birth.

Even in the Book of Tobit, "Within you, generations after generation shall proclaim their joy, and the name of her who is Elect shall endure through the generations to come." The gates of the city will be built of Sapphire and Emerald. (Tobit 13:11-12, 21)

Tobit was a descendant of Asaiah of Asiel of Seraiah of Naphtali.

"Daughter of Zion; for I am coming to dwell in the middle of you-it is Yahweh who speaks." (Zech. 2:4) It was Mary who gave birth to Our Savior, Our Immanuel, the upright one called Yashar'El. "Jeshurun whom I have chosen." (Is. 44:2) "One man will say, 'I belong to Yahweh', another will call himself by Jacob's name, on his hand another will write, "Yahweh" and be surnamed Israel." (Is. 44:5, Det. 33:26) Israel is Jacob.

It is important to follow the names of people, and there relationship to others, rather then when they reigned as King. The Book of Zechariah was not written by Zechariah, however, it gave a reference to the events occurring it in the times of King Uzziah. Even though it referenced to "King", doesn't mean that it was in the days of King Uzziah. For Zechariah's son was named Uzziah which puts them in the days of King David, not in the time frame of 782BCE of King Uzziah.

The children of Judah were Athaiah, son of Uzziah, son of Zechariah, the son of Amariah, son of Shephatiah, son of Mahalalel of the children of Perez. And Maaseiah the son of Baruch, the son of Colhozeh, son of Hazaiah, son of Adaiah, son of Joiarib, son of Zechariah, son of Shilonite. All the sons of Perez who lived in Jerusalem. Jedaiah, son of Joiarib. Seriah son of Hilkiah of Zadok of Levi. (Neh. 11:3-7, 1st Chrn. 6:46-50)

Just like the Book of Daniel was written around 167-164 BCE in kingdom of Greeks, doesn't mean that is when Daniel lived or that 167 is the actual date in history. For the reference to the kingdom of Greeks puts the years starting at least from 1000 BCE.

If you subtract the year 167 from 1000 = 833 BCE. Daniel is one of the sons of David who Habbakkuk took a meal to when in the lion's pit. Daniel is also known as Chileab, the second son of David and Abigail. (1st Sam. 3:2-5)

Daniel was actually deported to Babylon during one of the initial invasions by Pul of Assyria, and when Habbakkuk visited Daniel when in the lions pit was 80 years old. Habbakkuk was the son of the Shunammite woman in the time of Elisha. (2nd Kgs. 4:12-17)

Most people always referenced the time perimeter in the Book of Daniel to the destruction of the Temple. When most references to the destruction and desolation with 70 years of exile being described even in the Book of Tobit, and Daniel were referencing the desolation of the city of Jerusalem. "...as revealed by Yahweh to the prophet Jeremiah – that were to pass before the successive devastation of Jerusalem would come to a end, namely seventy years." (Dan. 9:1-3)

There were several people mentioned within antiquities that pertained to different events in history, as related in different books such as Book of Maccabees. Some of those names mentioned were Absalom, who is the son of King David, Mattithias, or called Mattithiah, the father of the Maccabees, Simeon, Judas, Simon, Jonathan, John, Eleazar, Jeremiah, Azariah, and Joseph. So how could these names being mentioned in what people believe to be in years of 167 BCE when they lived in antiquities of history. The confusion was that it was in years of the Kingdom of the Greeks which has its date perimeter starting 1000 BCE.

Even the mention of Menelaus of Sparta should direct you to the Kingdom of the Greeks for it was Menelaus who's wife was Helen of Troy. It was Helen of Troy that Paris the son of King Priam and Queen Hebuba, took Helen to be with him which caused the Trojan War. It was Alexander 1st who began the Hellenistic era, the Kingdom of Greeks started 1000 BCE.

Absalom was the son of King David and the rebellion and other wars were contained in the time frame of 867-837 BCE. With the rebellion being started in 843 BCE.

The Maccabees were the Hasmoneans during the Seleucid empire. The Rebellion was Absalom, and Mattithias father of Maccabees which is known as the Hasmonean revolt.

This war also engulfed Antiochus who wanted everyone to worship paganism, and who profaned the altar and sanctuary in Jerusalem. Mattithias Maccabeus, and is the son of Absalom. (1st Macc. 11:70 webc) Jonathan is the son of Absalom, and brother to Simon and Jonathan. (1st Macc. 5:17-18 webc)

Joseph was the son of Zechariah of Azariah. (1st Macc. 5:17-18 webc) but also Joseph was the son of Asaph of Jeroham. Zechariah's son was Uzziah, and Uzziah was known as Azariah. Eleazar who was called Avaran in the Book of Maccabees. (1st Macc. 6:43-44 webc) Eleazar is also the son of Phinehas (1st Chrn. 9:20, 2nd Sam. 18:17.9:10) also son of Dodo (2nd Sam. 23:9), and also Eliezar and Joash sons of Becher. (1st Chrn. 7:8)

It was Mattithias who was the son of Asaph, who is referred to in New Testament as Cleopas the husband of Martha.

In Jewish history Simeon is surnamed Cleopas. There was a man named Shimeon who was one of the sons of Harim. (Ez. 10:31) So Mariah could have been married to Shimeon, or wife to Simon who was the son of

Mattithias of Absalom the grandson of Simeon of Jacob. The very name of Mattithias in Hebrew is Antigonus. Mattithias son of John, son of Simeon priest of sons of Joarib. (1st Macc. 2:1) Joiarib son of Zechariah of Perez.

(Neh. 11:3-6) Mattithias son of John of Joiarib. (Neh. 12:11-21)

Heroides is Greek for Herod Antipater. Anipater father of Herod and was under Philip. Antipater the Idumaean father of Herod was the son of Jason in the time of Maccabees. (1st Macc 12:16, 14:22 webc)

(5th Macc. 33:1-4, 2nd Macc. 5:22-24 webc) Phillip was a Phrygian and sent Apollonius who was known as the lord of pollution to Jerusalem. Appolonius was the son of Thrasaeus the governor of Coele-Syria. Appolonius gather the gentiles to fight against the Maccabees and the Jews. (1st Macc. 3:10, 2nd Macc. 3:5 webc)

Alexander the Macedonian was the son of Philip, and Perseus who was King of Chittim. (1st Macc. 1:1, 8:5 webc, and Jasher 63:19-29, 62:25) The land and children of Chittim are the children of Africa. Zepho son of Eliphaz was the son of Esau who was made King of Chittim.

Most people don't even realize that Joseph, of Jacob was King of Egypt, and reigned for 80 years. (Jasher 59:20) Another fact is that Moses at age 18 fled Egypt to Cush. The King of Cush at that time was King Kikianus. Moses stayed there and at age 27 became King of Cush and reigned there for 40 years. (Jasher 72:2, 73:1-2) Cush are the Cushites/Kushites listed in the Book of Daniel. (11:44) And it was Ptolemy Philadelphus, son of Ptolemy 1st who defeated the Cush to gain their territory. (Gen. 10:6, 1st Chrn. 1:8) His wife was called Arsinoe, or called Cleopatra, the daughter of Lysimachus. (see Esther 11:1) Herodotus calls himself Apries, but in Greek spelling Herodotus is spelled Herodes, or Heroides. Jeremiah referred to him as Hophra. (Jer. 44:30)

Other historians put Hophra in a different timeline of dates.

(**Hophra is Hebrew name** but in **Greek Herodotus** called him **Apries who's reign ended around 664 BCE.....Hophra is son of Neco II** 664 BCE-595 BCE

Hophra is also the son of Psamtik 1st 690-664 BCE)

The abominations upon the altar was done in Greek year 145 or 855 BCE. Jerusalem was without inhabitants, and the sanctuary was broken down and strangers resided there. Judas fought the children of Esau in Indumea.. (1st Macc. 5:3, 56 webc) Joseph the son of Zacharias, and Azarias were remnants of the army in Judea while Simon went to Galilee. Even in the Lost Books of Bible Zechariah described seeing a man with a asses head upon him when he went into the Temple, and said "Woe, who do you worship." That ass was the anti-god, the ass of history!

The Maccabees when war ended cleansed the sanctuary of abominations, and the altar, and the dedication of the altar was for 8 days. (1st Macc. 4:56 webc)

"This day of the purification of the Temple fell on the very day on which the Temple had been profaned by the foreigners, the twenty-fifth of the same month, Chislev. They kept eight festal days with rejoicing, in the manner of the Feast of Tabernacles."

(2nd Macc. 10:5-6 webc)

Jonathan Priest in 7th month Greek year 160, or 840 BCE celebrated the **Feast of Tabernacles.** Under Simon's rule there was peace in the land, and they sat each man under his vine and his **fig tree.** (1st Macc. 14:12 webc) Same reference as to when Solomon became King there was **peace, and everyone sat under their own fig tree.**

The Fig trees main crop is between the months of August thru September. (1st Sam. 25:18)

Our Savior was born on the first day of Autumn which is September 25th.

It is also the Autumn time of year that Pomegranates are in abundance. Pomegranates were also used in the decoration of the pillar capitals, and High Priests robes. (Ex. 28:33-34) which symbolizes righteousness. Also Autumn is the season of Apples. "Under the apple tree I aroused you, there your mother conceived you, there she was in labor and bore you. Set me a seal on your heart, as a seal on your arm; for love is strong as death...Many waters can't quench love, neither can floods drown it. If a man would give all the wealth of his house for love." (Song. 8:5-7)

When He was born on earth a fountain would be open to them to help cleanse them of sin and impurity in order to have life. God Yahweh is the living water, and that a fountain shall flow out of Yahweh's house. (Joel 3:18) The light shines forth, and she has brought forth and delivered a child, a Savior in the time of the harvest. (Is. 9:6-7)

All the events in antiquities which led to the Birth of Our Savior, Our Immanuel took place before Solomon became King. For during these years there was deportations first into Egypt, then the Assyrians oppressed the Jews. (Is. 60:1-3, 6, 13 52:2-6)

"In those days and at that time I will cause a Branch of righteousness to grow up to David. He will execute justice and righteousness in the land. In those days Judah will be saved and Jerusalem will dwell safely. This is the name by which she will be called: Yahweh Our Righteousness." **The city will be built on the hill.** (Jer. 30:18 33:15-16, 23:5-6)

Yahweh came to earth in antiquities to save his flock, his children from sin in order to save their very souls. "He will destroy in this mountain the surface of the covering that covers all peoples, and the veil that is spread over all nations. He has swallowed up death forever! The Lord Yahweh will wipe away tears from off all faces." (Is. 25:7-8)

"It shall be said in that day, "Behold, this is our God! We have waited for him, and he will save us! This is Yahweh! We have waited for him. We will be glad and rejoice in his salvation! (Is. 25:9)

There is only one True God, one True Savior, and that is Yahweh. "I myself am Yahweh, besides me, there is no savior."

He came to earth out of love, and to teach people in the ways of love and to follow the light of Him to gain eternal life. I didn't want to write about the time of Jonah, but I was asked to write my feelings of His love.

When you love someone so much you want to protect them from being hurt in every way, including the hurt of their own soul from death. That is how God the Almighty Yahweh feels about his children. He raised you, taught you to love Him, and to keep his Covenant with Him. He knew that evil would try to lead many astray into sin and impurity. What evil had been doing made him angry from their perversions, abominations, and the influencing of his own people in the path of paganism.

Even today many are deceived by Constantine's New Testament books with his pagan logos name of Iesus, or spelled jesus. These churches over the centuries through repetition of that name deceived many into believing their falsehood as truth. People even try to justify the name by saying it is Yeshua, or Yehoshua, when both spellings are Joshua son of Nun. (Neh. 8:17) In Hebrew the word Yahusha means Father, and Yahuah means Salvation. Sir Isaac Newton proclaimed in his writings that the Anglican and Catholic churches and others did blasphemy in promoting the concept of the trinity, thereby violating the First Commandment of God Yahweh. "I AM Yahweh your God..You shall have no other gods before me." (Det. 5:6-7)

God was hurt that they didn't have the fidelity of love for Him as He did for them.

For some of these children turned away, and violated the very First Commandment of God to have no gods before him. Even the Blessed Mother Mary loves to the height of love. Even in the very beginning of Genesis it stated that She would crush the serpents head, and she did. (Gen. 3:14-15)

God knew that humans are not infallible, and that we do make mistakes. He was teaching his children to always walk in the light of His love, and not in the darkness of evil. He gave everyone the freedom to choose – the freedom to love, or to hate.

He wanted you to choose Him out of love to gain eternal life. He didn't want you to choose darkness by walking in the shadow of death with evil. He gave you the freedom of choice, for He didn't want to command you to love Him. He wanted you to freely love Him for who He is - a Father who has enduring love.

Evil has committed such abominations against humanity with the murdering of human beings, the very lives of adults, infants and children. How could anyone murder a child, and have no remorse, or empathy over what they do. How could anyone stand by, and not be affected by such inhumanity and disrespect for life. When a child is given, how could you not care about its existence, or its wanting to have life. How could anyone not be hurt over the death, the murder of innocence.

For everyone is someone's child, regardless of age, for even the elderly are someone's child. It is not right to abuse, torture, or murder human beings regardless of age.

In antiquities of the Bible these evil wanted to sacrifice human beings, even children in their ritual sacrifice to Moloch, which is just another name for murder.

How could you as a Father of Children stand by, and let your children be murdered by evil. To let them be led astray by evil into their perversions and abominable acts against humanity. Our Father could not let this happen to his children. So out of love for them He came to earth himself to teach, and to show them love. He taught them to walk in the righteous straight path of His love, and never to walk in the path of darkness.

He taught His children to keep his Commandments to save their own souls from death. Evil wanted to inflict such pain upon his chosen children in a effort to destroy their very life. They wanted to try to destroy everything related to God, simply out of such hatred for God, Our Father. They wanted to destroy life, the very city of life, and the very tree of life.

"I will tell of the loving kindness of Yahweh and the praises of Yahweh, according to all that Yahweh has given to us, and the great goodness toward the house of Israel, which he has given to them according to his mercies, and according to the multitude of his loving kindness. For he said, "Surely, they are my people, children who will not deal falsely; so he became their Savior. In all their affliction he was afflicted, and the angel of his presence saved them. In his love and in his pity he redeemed them. He bore them, and carried them all the days of old." (Is. 63:7-9)

As a Father who created you out of love, and held you in His arms from infancy, how could He stand by, and let evil try to destroy your life, the very souls He had made. God is not complacent in His love, but demonstrates how much He loves through the very action of love. If God never cared why would He send His prophets to warn people. If He didn't care why would He send His Holy Angels to watch over you, and comfort you.

Even when you felt so tired from fighting evil, and felt such despair, He gave you strength to continue. When your own heart was so broken He cradled you in his own arms to comfort you. If He didn't love you why would He come to earth himself to fight for you in order to save your very soul from death.

When He was on earth enduring all the things that you yourself were going through, how many stopped to comfort him in his sorrow. He endured much out of love for his own children. He bore their sorrow, and the sins being committed in order to save them from death. He could not endure such heartache over the abominations being committed against his own children that it crushed him so emotionally that the pain pierced to very center of him. He laid down his own life out of love, in which to save the very life of those He loved. By doing this unselfish Act of Love, He abolished death in which to save your very souls.

How many would come to the defense of the one True God Yahweh, who laid down his own life when on earth, in defense of you.

How many today would get on your knees to tell God how much you love Him.

How many would confess their sins, and never sin again, follow the path of His Ten Commandments, in which to gain eternal life with Him.

How many would even say "thank you" to God Yahweh for just loving you.

How many would even say to Yahweh, just three words, "I love you."

How many would freely love Him for who He is the Great I AM Amen Our Father, Yahweh.

The Hebrew prayer is:

Amen Our Father who art in Heaven,
Holy is Thy name,
Thy Kingdom come, Thy will be done
on earth as it is in Heaven.
Give us this day, our daily bread,
and forgive us our transgressions, as you
have forgiven others their transgressions.
And not to be led into temptation,
but deliver us from the evil one.
For thine is the Kingdom, the power, and all glory
forever, and ever Amen.

REFERENCE SECTION

All excerpted passages from Old Testament books as contained in:
World English Bible with Deuterocanonical/Apocryphal & Hebrew Names Version updated version of American Standard Version Bible, copyrighted, 1901 Philip Schaff translation, published by Thomas Nelson, N.Y. Public Domain

Jewish Masoretic Text, Jewish Publication Society of America, Philadelphia 1917 edition of the Hebrew Bible in English Public Domain

The Jerusalem Bible Reader's Edition, Copyrighted 1966, 1967, and 1968 by Darton, Longman & Todd Ltd and Doubleday & Company, Inc.

Karen Sobek: 2018 Meaning of The Great I Am as Amen, year calculations, timeline of events, dates of events, and year of return of captives, calculation & interpretation of Book of Daniel

Interpretation and transliteration of Hebrew letters contained in names referenced from the Hebrew alphabet where each letter of a name has further meaning.

Free On-Line Hebrew Cepher and Transliteration: Yahweh, Yashar'El, Immanuel
Hebrew to English Transliteration: Eliezer is Hebrew for Greek Lazarus, Elyon Most High God identified as Yahweh as in 2nd Samuel 22:14
Book of Yasher: sacred Texts
Testament of Simeon: Apocryphal Books from the Forgotten Books of Eden
Gospel of Mary: Apocryphal Books from the Forgotten Books of Eden
Athletes of Righteousness: Apocryphal Books, 4th Maccabees, Chapter 8
Simeon the Righteous: Jewish Knowledge

Chabad free Bible Dictionary: Hebrew timeline/Transliteration/Issaiah/Uzziah/Immanuel Chabad online: Timeline of Jewish History by Mattis Kantor

Jewish Encyclopedia: Mesoretic Text/ Star of David/Hannah
the mother of Samuel, Martha, Mary/Lennigrad codex/Zionist movement

Smith's Bible Dictionary, MCMXXXVII, Pub.By Barbour Publishing, Inc.P.O.Box 719, Uhrichsville, Ohio/ Martha & Mary/ Hannah/ Alexander/ Hycranus/ Aristobolus/ Apollonius/ Dionysius and other names.

The Human Search, John Lachs and Charles E. Scott, Oxford University Press, 1981
Philosophical works of John Locke/Power and Liberty

The Ayn Rand Lexicon, A Meridian Book, 1988, Vol.4: Socialism /UN/Capitalism/Collectivism

Britannica Encyclopedia on-line: Logos, Constantine, Roman history

Ancient Greek History Encyclopedia: Archaic period/ Classical/ Hellenistic/Trojan War/Ptolemy/ Hector and Paris and Helen of Troy/ Alexander and Cleopatra of Macedonia/Menelaus/Claudias
Alexander the Great and Cleopatra of Macedonia, Homer: Peloponnesian war

Wikipedia on-line/Paris of Troy
New World Encyclopedia/Ancient Greece
Livius/articles on-line: Cleopatra of Macedonia
Wikipedia on-line: Ptolemaic Kingdom

Wikipedia on-line reference source:
Messiah in Judism/Prophets in Judaism/ List of High Priests of Israel/Chronology
Jewish Calendar/Prophet Isaiah/Iddo Prophet/Isaiah/Uzziah/Zerubbable/Messiah
in Judaism/Timeline of Jerusalem/Logos pagan cult of Constantine
of the Bible Eusebius and Constantine/Biblical Text Criticism/ Logos/Missing years

Wikipedia on-line/ reference/Anno Mundi and Jewish tradition/Hebrew and Athenian lunar calendars/ Alexandrian era/ Seleucid/ Roman Julian Calendar and months/Gregorian/Greek/ Babylonian Calendar/ Macedonian Calendar

CPSIA information can be obtained
at www.ICGtesting.com
Printed in the USA
BVHW021110100919
557929BV00024B/11/P